INDY CAFE COOKBOOK

VOLUME 2

CREATE A SLICE OF CAFE CULTURE AT HOME

INDY CAFE COOKBOOK

Publisher: Salt Media

Editor: Selena Young

Copy editors/proof readers: Kathryn Lewis, Melissa Morris, Jo Rees, Rosanna Rothery, Melissa Stewart

Production manager: Tamsin Powell

Production assistant: Charlotte Cummins

Art direction and design: Christopher Mulholland

Photography: Matt Austin 120, 194; John Eldridge 126, 128, 202; Guy Harrop 8, 28, 32, 65, 108, 185, 193; Tom Kahler 148; Steve Lovatt 151; SLR Photography 112, 115, 116, 119; Joan Ransley 90, 107; Gavin Smart 186

indycoffee.guide

ISBN 9781916085923

First published in Great Britain in 2022 by Salt Media Ltd

Text © 2022 Salt Media Ltd

Design and layout © 2022 Salt Media Ltd

Printed in Great Britain

www.saltmedia.co.uk
01271 859299
ideas@saltmedia.co.uk

The right of Salt Media to be identified as the author of this work has been asserted by it in accordance with the Copyright, Designs and Patents Act 1988.

A catalogue record of the book is available from the British Library.

All rights reserved. No part of this publication may be reproduced, distributed, or transmitted in any form or by any means, including photocopying, recording, or other electronic or mechanical methods, without the prior written permission of the publisher, except in the case of brief quotations embodied in critical reviews and certain other non-commercial uses permitted by copyright law.

For permission requests, email Salt Media.

While every effort has been made to ensure the accuracy of the information in this publication, we cannot be held responsible for any errors or omissions and take no responsibility for the consequences of error or for any loss or damage suffered by users of any of the information published on any of these pages.

CONTENTS

EVOLUTION OF THE SPECIALITY CAFE	12
COFFEE GUIDE	26
BREAKFAST & BRUNCH	29
LUNCH & SUPPER	91
BAKES, CAKES & DESSERTS	125
DRINKS	173
THE PLAYLIST	204
INDEX	206

Routinely pick up freshly made loaves of springy sourdough from your fave cafe-bakery? Devoted fan of your local coffee shop's cakes and brunches? This is the cookbook for you.

In the second edition of the *Indy Cafe Cookbook*, the *Independent Coffee Guide* team have left no doughnut unturned in the search for the best brunch dishes, luscious lunches, creative bakes and coffee-infused drinks.

The curation of easy-to-recreate signature dishes comes from the kitchens of 40 of the UK's hero speciality cafes and roasteries. Every recipe has been matched with a coffee and playlist pairing so you can create a slice of cafe culture at home.

ENJOY!

Indy Coffee Guide team

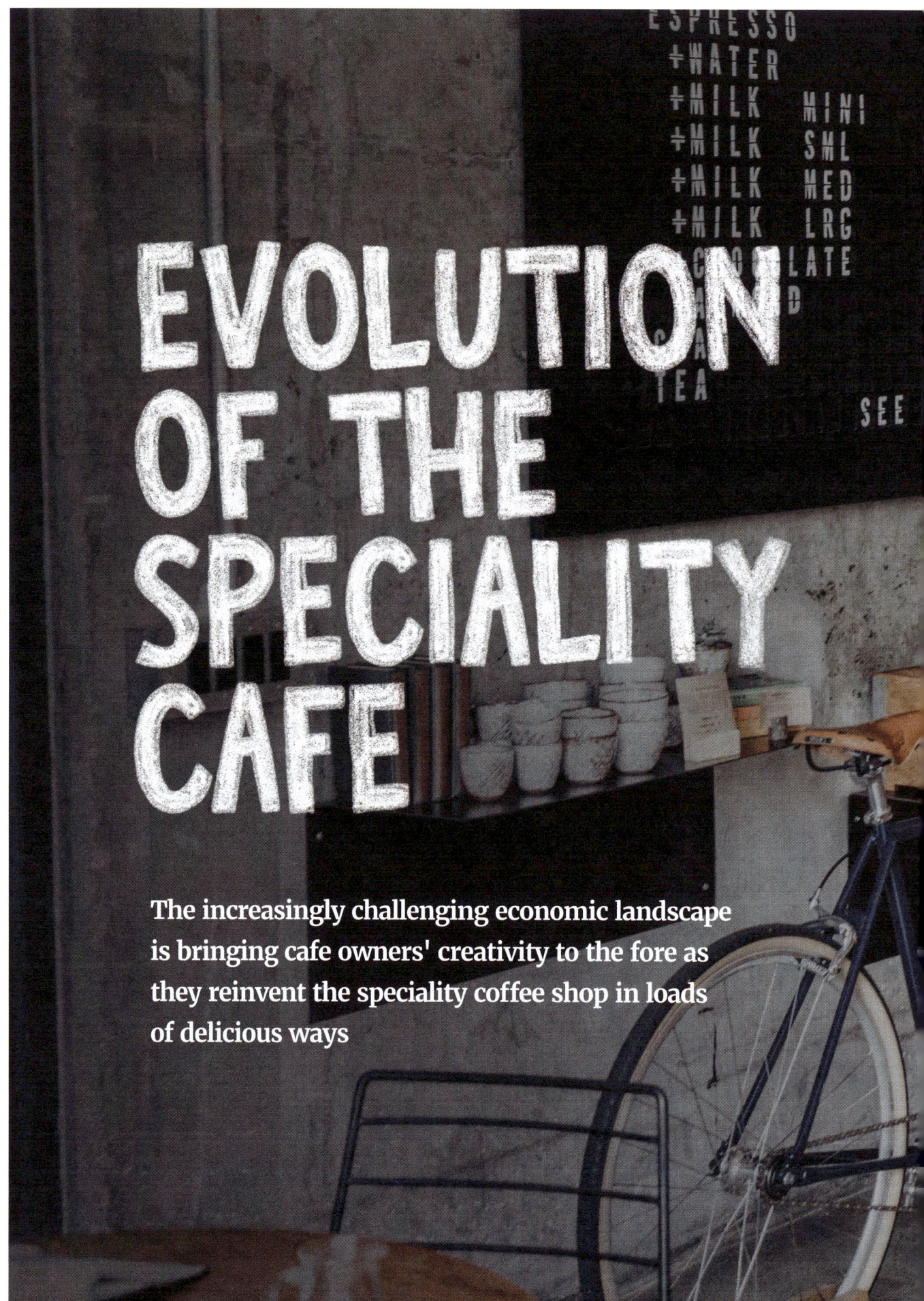

EVOLUTION OF THE SPECIALITY CAFE

The increasingly challenging economic landscape is bringing cafe owners' creativity to the fore as they reinvent the speciality coffee shop in loads of delicious ways

The UK's coffee culture is in an unprecedented period of change and development as a result of Brexit, Covid and a number of other challenges.

During the lockdowns, coffee shops, cafes and roasteries explored and fast-tracked new ventures in order to stay afloat. Customers rallied around (and relied upon) their favourite indie coffee shops as a source of spirit-lifting caffeine fixes and takeout treats.

Some venues started doing takeaway food for the first time, which proved to be so popular that they've kept it as another string to their bow. Casual cafe dishes now vie with popular restaurants on takeout platforms such as Just Eat and Deliveroo.

The shift in the coffeesphere has resulted in a flurry of new openings and cafe incarnations. One of the most exciting has been the burgeoning rise of cafe-bakery hybrids, where superb sourdough and next-level doughnuts are paired with top-notch brews.

Another seductive development has been the rise of after-hours cafes where, come dusk, flat whites and croissants are ditched for cocktails and small plates. And, of course, there's been an explosion of roastery cafes where visitors can watch beans being bronzed while sipping a brew crafted from the latest freshly roasted batch. Let's take a closer look …

OWN-ROASTED BEANS

Don Iszatt, founder of the Finca group of cafes in Dorset and Somerset, started roasting coffee in a wok at home before he opened the first Finca outpost (in Dorchester) in 2014. He was surprised to discover that his own-roasted beans were easily a match for coffee he could source elsewhere so, once he'd opened the cafe, he bought a small roaster and started bronzing beans to serve to his customers.

In-house roasting has given Don the opportunity to manage all stages of the coffee production – from bean to cup. He says: *'We could buy speciality-grade coffee from a number of roasteries, but they control the quality, consistency and accountability. By doing it ourselves we know exactly where the coffee is from and how fresh it is.'*

There are other, softer, benefits too: *'It brings customers closer to the coffee process, something they won't find in commodity chains like Starbucks,'* he explains.

Another cafe owner who sidestepped into the world of roasting is Robi Lambie, founder of Cairngorm Coffee in Edinburgh.

When Robi opened his second coffee shop in the city in 2016, he realised that roasting the coffee himself would be commercially beneficial while also heightening his customers' experiences.

'It was about trying to build something that extended beyond the four walls of our cafe. Beyond the romance of roasting and then selling your own beans, it's also exciting to have a tangible product which people can take home and experience outside of the cafe. We're a part of their day, even when they're not in the coffee shop.'

Conversely, it's becoming increasingly common for roasteries such as Dark Woods in Huddersfield and Fire & Flow in Cirencester to create roastery cafes or use their space for pop-up cafe events and tasting sessions.

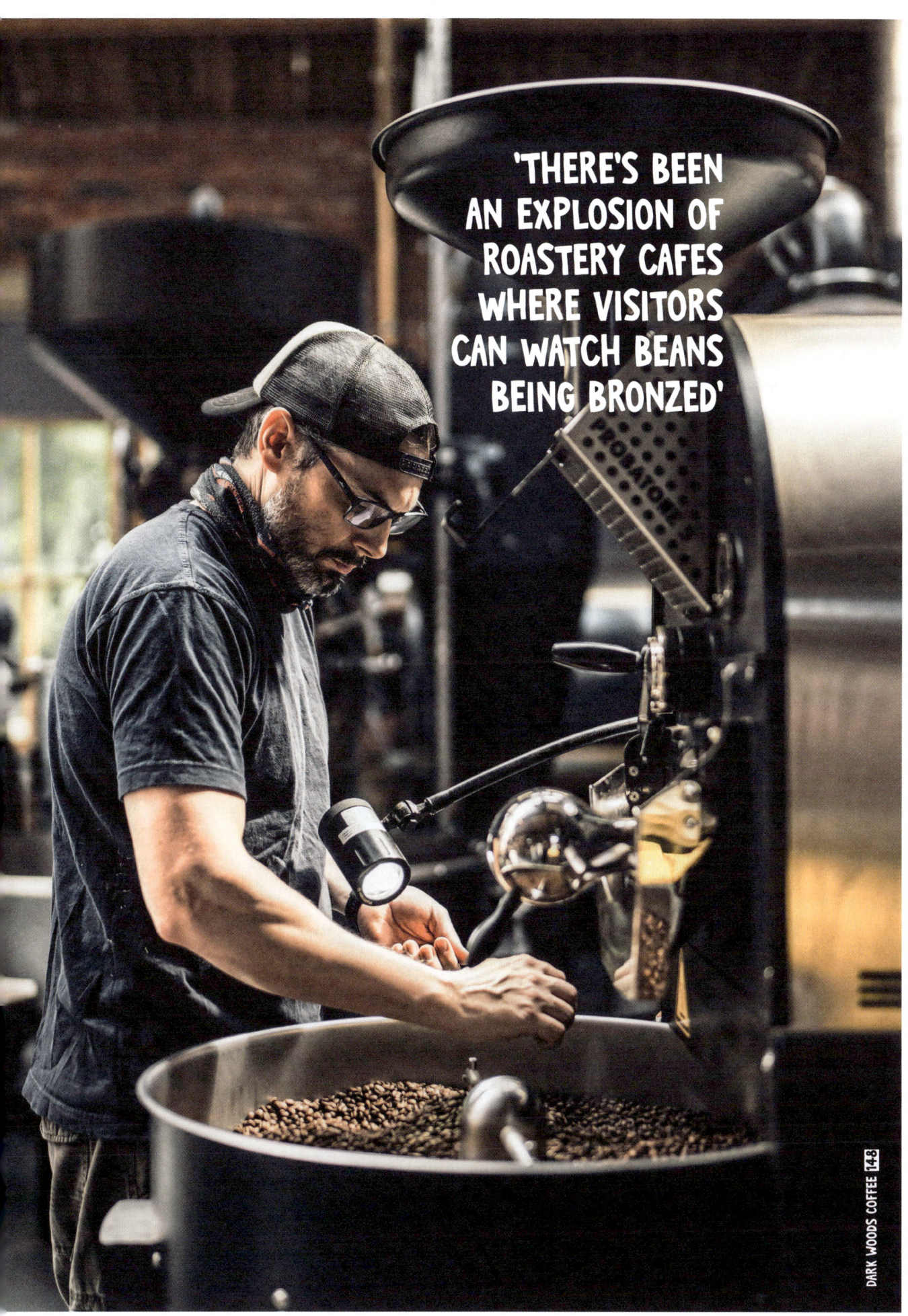

PLANT POWER

Another development in the speciality cafe scene is how mainstream vegan food has become. Things have moved on a lot from the time when the only milk served in coffee shops came from cows, and 'vegan food' generally meant lacklustre flapjacks.

Exeter's Sacred Grounds has been at the forefront of the city's vegan dining scene since it opened in 2018 and distinguished itself as a go-to for plant-based cafe dining.

Co-owner Hayley Maker recalls the uninspiring local vegan scene that existed before she and her co-owners Becca Allen and Nathan Maker set up shop. She says: *'As vegans, we were only too aware of the lack of vegan dining options in the area. So we set out to create a place where people like us could experience delicious seasonal plant-based food. We also wanted to shine a light on regional produce because we weren't seeing that locally.*

'As we're in the niche business of being completely plant-based, we also wanted to open people's minds to how good vegan food can be.'

To achieve this, the trio enlisted the help of a pro chef. Hayley says: *'Our early collaboration with a creative chef gave us the wow factor from the get-go. He set a standard for our menus, which we've worked hard to continuously elevate and refine.'*

The cafe's innovative dishes have attracted diners of all persuasions and even won over cynics.

'Most of our customers aren't vegan or vegetarian, but they come here because they know the food and drink will be good. Of course, there are those who are sceptical about vegan-only brunches and baffled by our vegan eggs but, once they try them, they love them.'

It's not only plant-based dishes that have proved popular: alt milks have also gone stratospheric. Hayley says: *'People are far more aware of alternative milks now. When we opened, customers were shocked to find we didn't offer dairy milk, but now alternatives are mainstream.*

'The alternative milks have improved and some pair beautifully with coffee. This is, of course, also testament to roasteries like Roastworks Coffee Co. in Devon that roast delicious beans for us to match with non-dairy milks,' says Hayley.

Robi of Cairngorm has also experienced massive demand for alt milks, and says: *'Our oat milk sales are through the roof. Probably a third of our coffee trade is oat-based, which is pretty crazy.'*

CAFE-BAKERY HYBRIDS

Those who like to pair their coffee with a sweet side will have been delighted by the recent boom in cafe bakeries. They're the kind of places where you can sip a well-crafted coffee and chow down on toothsome carbs which, sometimes, have both been made from scratch on-site.

Finca was one of the trailblazing cafes that led this particular field and its Poundbury bakehouse now supplies high-calibre carbs to the four Finca cafes.

'We didn't want to buy cakes from other suppliers because we wanted to be in control of the production,' says founder Don.

'We source the raw ingredients which means we know exactly where they come from and can change the variables to get every recipe just right. It takes extra resource, skill, time, space and energy but it's really important.'

While delivering delicious sustenance, these cafe bakeries also give their customers a delightful sensory experience while they sip and munch. This includes inhaling the scent of hot-from-the-oven bread and just-ground coffee while enjoying the visual thrill of watching talented bakers craft goods before their eyes.

'When someone comes into our Poundbury cafe and sees the ovens in the background they automatically make the connection between what they're ordering and what's being baked,' says Don. *'Before they eat a cinnamon bun they can watch them being prepped and chat with the bakers about them – it's unique.'*

The carbs are as important as the coffee in spots such as Town Mill Bakery in Lyme Regis, Dorset and Electric Bakery in Bude, Cornwall, which draw crowds for their droolworthy breads and pastries. Kookaburra Bakehouse in Chester has even earned a rep specifically for its handmade cruffins, which ooze with next-level flavours such as lemon meringue and strawberry cheesecake mousse.

CHOCOLATE ALMOND CROISSANT

AFTER-HOURS CAFES

Noticed more people hanging out in coffee venues post-5pm? It's odds on they're waiting for the cafe to roll into its evening guise as a spot for drinks and dinner.

More cafe and coffee shop owners are using their spaces to welcome punters for after-hours fun. The introduction of coffee cocktails, craft beer and nitro cold brew, alongside cafe food that's turned up a notch, is resulting in evening cafes giving conventional bars a run for their money.

It's something Sacred Grounds initially experimented with via its monthly supper clubs and now regularly runs as its Sacred Nights.

'We wanted to add something different, relaxed and informal to Exeter's night-time economy,' says Hayley. *'Sacred Nights centre around a menu of small plates, each paired with beautiful natural wines and cocktails.'*

These day-to-night spaces pair perfectly with the growing popularity of unfussy but quality food served in casual settings.

'We're fortunate as our space is versatile and it feels different from day to night,' says Hayley. *'In the evening we decorate the outside dining area with foliage and it's lit by candlelight which makes it feel quite intimate.'*

Keeping the party going past 5pm also adds another revenue stream for indie businesses operating in a challenging economic climate. Hayley says: *'It's brilliant that cafes can adapt and diversify what they offer, especially to attract a new audience. Our daytimes have been boosted because of the evening service – it's made us more visible. It's great they've been popular because it's a difficult time for independent cafes.'*

FUTURE-PROOFING

In addition to independent coffee shop owners exploring roasting, bolstering their food offering with own-made treats and extending their opening hours, what else can we expect to come over the horizon?

'I think cafe owners will continue to diversify in order to stand out, perhaps through pourover stations or similar new additions to their spaces. We've just put a nitro cold brew machine in our cafe to inject a bit more life into the cafe experience,' says Robi.

'We're also going to see more venues opening. Many people spent the pandemic rethinking their office jobs and are chasing the dream of being cafe owners.'

Don predicts that more cafes and roasteries will take control of the food and drink they serve: *'We're going to see an increase in roastery cafes because there's a lot of support for that from consumers. Hopefully there'll also be more signs saying "Coffee roasted down the road" and cafes producing their own baked goods.'*

He's also got his money on plant-based food options being the norm: *'We're going to see more vegan dishes on menus; there's already an increase in demand from people who aren't even vegan.'*

It's a forecast Hayley agrees with: *'Since we opened there's been a real evolution in the vegan scene, with an emergence of great places to eat out. I think that will continue to grow.'*

Supporting local independent cafes is essential if we want to enjoy the benefits they offer. Robi of Cairngorm says: *'Cafes play a huge role in bringing together people from local and like-minded communities and they become an important part of our daily lives.'*

We'll raise a cold brew to that.

COFFEE GUIDE

Don't know your cortardo from your Chemex?
Callum Parsons of Fire & Flow Coffee Roasters breaks down the brews

ESPRESSO DRINKS

ESPRESSO

A concentrate of coffee created by pushing water, at pressure, through finely ground beans.

AMERICANO

Espresso diluted with hot water to reduce strength to taste.

FLAT WHITE

Espresso topped with velvety steamed milk. Served in a 6–8oz cup for the best balance of milk to coffee.

CAPPUCCINO

Espresso with a thicker foam to give a fuller mouthfeel. Served in a 6–8oz cup with an optional dusting of cocoa.

CORTADO

An equal measure of espresso to steamed milk 1:1. Served in a 4oz cup.

PICCOLO

Espresso with steamed milk served in a 3.5oz glass tumbler.

LATTE

Espresso with silky steamed milk. Drink size of 10–12oz results in a more muted coffee flavour than a flat white.

FILTER BREW METHODS

FRENCH PRESS/CAFETIERE

Freshly ground beans and hot water are brewed together in the base of the cafetiere for 3-4 minutes. Any foam is then removed from the top, the filter is plunged and the coffee poured.

SYPHON

Creating steam in the bottom chamber forces and keeps water in the top chamber where the ground coffee is added. When the brewing process is complete, the heat source is turned off and the brewed coffee drops through a filter back into the bottom.

V60

An individual pourover method that's placed over a cup. A choice of filter (paper, metal or cloth) is placed in the funnel of the V60, then freshly ground coffee added and hot water poured over. The coffee drips into the cup.

AEROPRESS

Coffee is placed in the top chamber and hot water added. After 2 minutes of brewing, the AeroPress is slowly plunged. Pressure forces the steeped liquid through the filter and into a cup.

CHEMEX

Filter paper is placed in the funnel of the Chemex, ground coffee is added and hot water poured over. After steeping, the filter and coffee grounds are removed, leaving the coffee ready to pour.

COLD BREW

Ground coffee is steeped in cold water for anything between 15-20 hours to create a concentrate which is diluted to taste and served chilled.

NITRO COLD BREW

Cold brew infused with nitrogen and pulled through a draught tap to add creaminess.

CREAMY MUSHROOMS ON TOAST

BREAKFAST & BRUNCH

RHUBARB CRUMBLE WAFFLES	32
SWEET POTATO FRITTERS WITH SMASHED AVOCADO, HALLOUMI AND POACHED EGGS	38
SMOKED HADDOCK BAKED EGGS IN A LEMON, NUTMEG AND MUSTARD SAUCE	41
GRANARY SUNSHINE TOAST	44
TURKISH EGGS	48
NUTTY GRANOLA WITH MANGO COMPOTE	52
SWEET POTATO HASH	56
VEGGIE FRITTATA	60
CREAMY MUSHROOMS ON TOAST	64
SACRED SCRAMBLED TOFU	68
TIRAMISU FRENCH TOAST	72
EGGY CRUMPETS WITH CHILLI JAM AND HALLOUMI	76
SMOKED HADDOCK POTATO CAKES WITH KALE PESTO AND POACHED EGGS	80
THAI YELLOW EGGS WITH MANGO CHUTNEY AND SALTED CUCUMBER	84
CRUMPETS WITH SLOW-COOKED PORTOBELLO MUSHROOMS, BEETROOT RELISH AND ROCKET PESTO	88

JOURNEY SOCIAL KITCHEN

Lancaster, Lancashire

Journey Social is a brunch institution in Lancaster, so its regulars were pretty jazzed when this sister outpost opened on New Street in 2021. Whether you settle inside the contemporary cafe or head to the bijou outdoor area, there's plenty of room to roadtest dishes from its droolworthy brunch menu.

Highlights include the JS staple of stacked-to-the-max french toast and the house fave of steak and eggs. Everything is made from scratch and with a healthy dollop of care and attention.

Similar dedication to doing things properly is poured into the coffee offering. New Zealand's Allpress supplies the beans that are prepared as top-notch espresso and filter brews.

RECIPE
RHUBARB CRUMBLE WAFFLES

RHUBARB CRUMBLE WAFFLES

CHEF'S TIP: 'DON'T OWN A WAFFLE IRON? THIS RECIPE WORKS WELL WITH PANCAKES OR EVEN SHOP-BOUGHT WAFFLES'

COFFEE PAIRING

Flat white

PLAYLIST PAIRING

Song: Orange Sky
Artist: Alexi Murdoch

RHUBARB CRUMBLE WAFFLES

Recipe by Jeff Marshall of Journey Social Kitchen

Serves **4**
Preparation time **20 minutes**
Cooking time **1 hour**

You will need

Waffle iron
Silicone moulds (we use half-sphere moulds) 4

For the crumble

Oats 125g
Unsalted butter 15g, at room temperature
Muscovado sugar 50g
Golden syrup 50g

For the poached rhubarb and rhubarb jelly

Rhubarb 500g, cut into 8cm pieces
Orange 1, zest and juice
Caster sugar 100g
Agar-agar powder

For the gooseberry puree

Gooseberries 200g
Caster sugar 35g

For the crème anglaise

Double cream 235ml
Vanilla extract 10ml
Free-range egg yolks 4
Caster sugar 65g

For the waffles

Plain flour 250g, sieved
Salt 1 tsp
Baking powder 4 tsp
White sugar 2 tbsp
Free-range eggs 2 medium
Milk 350ml, warmed
Butter 75g, melted
Vanilla extract 1 tsp

1. *For the crumble:* preheat the oven to 180°C / gas 4. Evenly spread the oats on a large baking tray and bake for 10–12 minutes, stirring halfway through, until they are toasted and golden.

2. In a small saucepan, gently melt the butter with the sugar and golden syrup until the sugar has dissolved. Carefully pour the mixture over the oats and give it a good mix. Place the oats back in the oven for 20 minutes, until golden brown and crunchy.

3. *For the poached rhubarb and rhubarb jelly:* put the rhubarb, orange zest and juice, and 2 tbsp of water in a saucepan. Bring to the boil then leave to gently simmer for 10 minutes.

4. Remove the rhubarb from its liquid and set the fruit aside. Turn up the heat to reduce the liquid by half.

5. Weigh the reduced liquid then add 1.3g of agar-agar for every 100g of liquid. Simmer for a further 5 minutes then remove from the heat. Allow to cool then pour into moulds and put in the fridge to set.

6. *For the gooseberry puree:* put the gooseberries and sugar in a saucepan over a low heat. Once the gooseberries break down and the mixture starts to boil, cook for 5 minutes or until the skins are soft. Put the mixture in a blender and blitz to a puree.

7. *For the crème anglaise:* in a small saucepan, heat the cream and vanilla until bubbles form.

8. While the cream heats, whisk together the egg yolks and sugar until smooth.

9. Slowly pour around 100ml of the hot cream mixture into the egg yolks, whisking continuously. Then slowly add the egg yolk mixture into the remaining cream mixture in the saucepan, whisking continuously. Return the saucepan to the heat and stir continuously until the mixture coats the back of a spoon.

10. *For the waffles:* preheat the waffle iron. In a large bowl, mix all of the dry ingredients together.

11. In another bowl, beat the eggs, then stir in the milk, butter and vanilla. Pour the egg mixture into the flour mixture and beat until smooth.

12. Fill the waffle iron with batter. Cook the waffles until golden and crisp.

13. Serve the waffles with the poached rhubarb, rhubarb jelly, gooseberry puree, crème anglaise and a sprinkle of crumble.

Bean Loved

Skipton, Yorkshire

Serving top-notch flat whites and long blacks since 2007, Bean Loved was the first speciality cafe in Skipton and continues its mission to champion delicious and responsibly sourced coffee.

Rather than offering a menagerie of brewing methods and beans, founder Wes Bond focuses on producing consistently spot-on espresso using a bespoke house blend from Dark Woods Coffee in Huddersfield.

It's not just coffee that Wes and head chef Alastair Fox are passionate about, as food is where the team really let their creativity fly. Bean Loved's menu of brunch and lunch dishes is one of the best for miles.

RECIPES

SWEET POTATO FRITTERS WITH SMASHED AVOCADO, HALLOUMI AND POACHED EGGS

&

SMOKED HADDOCK BAKED EGGS IN A LEMON, NUTMEG AND MUSTARD SAUCE

Sweet Potato Fritters with Smashed Avocado, Halloumi and Poached Eggs

Recipe by Alastair Fox of Bean Loved

Serves **2**
Preparation time **25–30 minutes**
Cooking time **10 minutes**

For the sweet potato fritters

Red onion ½, peeled and diced
Garlic 1 clove, peeled and chopped
Ground nutmeg ½ tsp
Ground cloves ½ tsp
Piquanté peppers 2 tsp, chopped
Sweet potatoes 2 large, peeled and grated
Free-range egg 1
Double cream 1 tbsp
Self-raising flour (plus extra for dusting) 90g
Vegetable oil for frying

For the smashed avocado

Ripe avocado 1, peeled and pitted
Lime 1, zest and juice
Fresh coriander 1 tbsp, chopped

For the sriracha mayonnaise

Mayonnaise 100g
Sriracha sauce 25g

To serve

Halloumi 2 thick slices, fried
Free-range eggs 2, poached
Chilli jam 2 tsp
Chilli flakes 2 tsp

1. *For the fritters:* sauté the onion and garlic in a non-stick frying pan over a medium heat. Add the nutmeg, cloves and piquanté peppers until cooked through. Transfer into a large mixing bowl, add the grated sweet potato and combine.

2. In a separate bowl, combine the egg, cream and flour to form a wet dough. Add to the sweet potato mixture and combine until the dough has completely broken down. Add 1 tbsp of flour and mix again. Season and then refrigerate for 10–15 minutes.

3. Remove the fritter mixture from the fridge. Gently shape the mixture into 4 golf-ball-size fritters, patting each down to 2½cm thickness. Shallow fry in hot oil for 2–3 minutes on either side, or until golden brown.

4. *For the smashed avocado:* put the avocado and lime zest and juice in a bowl. Mash the avocado with the back of a fork. Stir the coriander through the avocado, season to taste and set aside.

5. *For the sriracha mayonnaise:* put the mayonnaise and sriracha in a bowl and stir to combine.

6. *To serve:* place a fritter in the centre of each plate and layer with halloumi, smashed avocado, another fritter and then top with a poached egg. Drizzle the stack with sriracha mayonnaise and garnish to taste with chilli jam and flakes.

CHEF'S TIP:
'CARNIVORES CAN SWAP FRIED HALLOUMI FOR CRISP SLICES OF CHORIZO'

COFFEE PAIRING
Flat white

PLAYLIST PAIRING
Song: We Don't Funk
Artist: KIRBY

PLAYLIST PAIRING

Song: You Ain't the Problem

Artist: Michael Kiwanuka

COFFEE PAIRING

Cortado

CHEF'S TIP: 'TRY ADDING A SPLASH OF WHITE WINE TO THE SAUCE'

SMOKED HADDOCK BAKED EGGS IN A LEMON, NUTMEG AND MUSTARD SAUCE

Recipe by Alastair Fox of Bean Loved

Serves **2**
Preparation time **10–15 minutes**
Cooking time **8–10 minutes**

For the lemon, nutmeg and mustard sauce

Butter 25g
Plain flour 25g
Milk 250ml
Lemon 1, zest and juice
Ground nutmeg ½ tsp
Wholegrain mustard 1 tsp

Spinach leaves 20g
Smoked haddock 100g, sliced
Free-range eggs 4
Emmental 40g, grated
Sourdough 2 slices, toasted

1. *For the lemon, nutmeg and mustard sauce:* gently melt the butter in a saucepan, then add the flour and stir to create a smooth roux. Slowly add the milk – ensuring each pour is absorbed into the roux before adding more – until you have a smooth and creamy sauce. Add the lemon zest and juice, nutmeg and mustard. Combine and season to taste.

2. Preheat the oven to 180°C / gas 4. Warm 2 small ovenproof serving dishes in the oven. Remove from the oven and fill each with spinach leaves and smoked haddock. Completely cover with the mustard sauce. Top each with 2 raw eggs.

3. Place in the oven and bake for 5 minutes. Remove from the oven and top with the emmental, then bake for a further 3-4 minutes until the egg whites are cooked but the yolks are still runny. Serve with toasted sourdough.

GRANARY CAFE

Linlithgow, West Lothian

David Stein and his family own businesses across Scotland, including butcher shops, restaurants and bars. They took over Granary Cafe in 2020 with the aim of building on its already sterling reputation for quality food and drink in Linlithgow – which they've done in style.

The vibrant cafe is a popular spot with tourists who swing by for a morning coffee paired with a slice of homemade traybake, or who linger over lunch between visits to the loch and the magnificent ruins of Linlithgow Palace.

Recommended faves include the flat white made with quality beans from Glen Lyon, which pairs perfectly with Granary Cafe's baked eggs with salmon, avocado and cheddar.

RECIPE
GRANARY SUNSHINE TOAST

GRANARY SUNSHINE TOAST

Recipe by Lia Teixeira of Granary Cafe

Serves **1**
Preparation time **10 minutes**
Cooking time **5 minutes**

Chorizo sausage 1 small, halved
Vegetable oil 1 tbsp
Free-range egg 1 large
Salt and pepper to season

To serve

Sourdough 1 thick slice
Spring onion 1, sliced
Dill a small handful, roughly chopped
Aleppo pepper a large pinch

1. Cook the chorizo for 3–4 minutes under a hot grill. Alternatively, fry in a griddle pan over a high heat for 2 minutes on each side.

2. While the chorizo cooks, heat the oil in a small frying pan and fry the egg until the edges are crisp. Toast the sourdough.

3. *To assemble:* place the sourdough on a plate and top with the fried egg. Place the chorizo halves on the side. Dress with the spring onion and sprinkle liberally with dill and aleppo pepper.

COFFEE PAIRING

Glen Lyon Coffee Roasters Red Stag Blend latte

PLAYLIST PAIRING

Song: Last of the Loving
Artist: Coco

CHEF'S TIP: 'MAKE THIS EVEN MORE INDULGENT BY ADDING A DOLLOP OF LABNEH OR THICK GREEK YOGURT, OR DRIZZLING WITH MELTED BUTTER MIXED WITH ALEPPO PEPPER'

TOWN MILL BAKERY

Lyme Regis, Dorset

The rise of bakery cafes over the last decade is a food trend that's hopefully here to stay, especially when they're as good as this Lyme Regis hangout.

Visitors, whether sitting at one of the sociable refectory-style tables or picking up goods to-go, are greeted by the intoxicating scent of freshly ground coffee followed by the arresting aroma of hot-from-the-oven bread. Once your nose is over the Town Mill Bakery threshold, there's no choosing one over the other.

Crisp, golden pastries tempt visitors to indulge in a quick sugar and caffeine combo, but it's well worth making time to linger over brunch and lunch dishes from the all-day menu.

RECIPE
TURKISH EGGS

TURKISH EGGS

Recipe by Wojciech Borecki of Town Mill Bakery

Serves **2**
Preparation time **30 minutes**
Cooking time **10 minutes**

For the chilli butter

Unsalted butter 200g
Olive oil 20ml
Smoked paprika 1 tsp
Chilli flakes 1½ tsp
Sea-salt flakes to season

For the dukkah

Sesame seeds 1½ tsp
Fennel seeds 1 tsp
Cumin seeds 1 tsp
Coriander seeds 2 tbsp
Hazelnuts 40g
Almonds 40g
Pistachios 40g
Cayenne pepper or paprika ½ tsp
Sea-salt flakes a pinch

For the dill yogurt

Greek yogurt 180g
Dill 10g, chopped
Chives 10g, chopped
Sea-salt flakes 1 tsp
Paprika 1½ tsp
Garlic powder 1½ tsp
Olive oil 10ml

To serve

Free-range eggs 4, poached
Fresh herbs to taste
Sourdough sliced and toasted
Avocado peeled, pitted and sliced

1. *For the chilli butter:* melt the butter in a heavy-based saucepan over a very low heat. Discard the separated milk solids that rise to the top, leaving the transparent golden liquid. Don't rush this step, it will take around 15–20 minutes.

2. Allow the clarified butter to cool in the pan, then add the olive oil. Stir in the paprika, chilli flakes and sea salt. Mix well and set aside.

3. *For the dukkah:* in a pan, gently toast the seeds until lightly coloured and fragrant. Allow to cool before transferring to a large pestle and mortar. Add the remaining dukkah ingredients and pound until crushed (alternatively, use a spice grinder).

4. *For the dill yogurt:* mix all the ingredients together and spoon into the centre of 2 breakfast bowls.

5. Gently warm the chilli butter while poaching the eggs.

6. *To serve:* place the eggs on top of the dill yogurt, drizzle with chilli butter and sprinkle with dukkah and fresh herbs to taste. Serve with a couple of slices of avocado and toasted sourdough.

CHEF'S TIP: 'THE CHILLI BUTTER CAN BE MADE IN ADVANCE AND WILL KEEP IN THE FRIDGE FOR 1–2 WEEKS. DUKKAH CAN BE STORED IN AN AIRTIGHT CONTAINER FOR 2–3 WEEKS'

COFFEE PAIRING

Extract Cast Iron short black

PLAYLIST PAIRING

Song: (Sittin' on) the Dock of the Bay

Artist: Otis Redding

MERAKI COFFEE CO.

Woolacombe, Devon

No two visits to this north Devon hangout are never quite the same. Whether it's a new guest roast on the second grinder, fresh finds on the food menu or the ever-changing local artwork and photography on the walls, there's always something novel to inspire.

Thanks to its spot on a side street just off Woolacombe's incredible beach, Meraki's loyal local following is supplemented by a stream of tourists who seek it out for speciality coffee by the sea. Its proximity to the shore influences its laid-back vibe: sandy-toed beachgoers queue for coffee, surfboards are propped outside and dogs snooze by the woodburner after walks through the dunes.

RECIPE

NUTTY GRANOLA WITH MANGO COMPOTE

NUTTY GRANOLA WITH MANGO COMPOTE

Recipe by Molly Hutchings of Meraki Coffee Co.

Serves **10**
Preparation time **30 minutes**
Cooking time **30 minutes**

For the granola

Coconut oil 125ml
Maple syrup 125ml
Ground cinnamon 1 tsp
Salt ½ tsp
Rolled oats 240g
Pumpkin seeds 50g
Hazelnuts 50g
Flaked almonds 35g

For the mango compote

Frozen mango 350g
Sugar 1½ tsp
Lemon ¼, juice
Water 70ml

Additional toppings (per bowl)

Banana ½, peeled and sliced
Blackberries a small handful
Yogurt 1 tbsp
Coconut flakes a sprinkle
Flaked almonds a sprinkle
Chia seeds a sprinkle

1. *For the granola:* preheat the oven to 140°C / gas 1.
2. Line a large baking tray with baking parchment. Put the coconut oil in a heat-proof bowl and put it in the oven for 2–4 minutes until the oil has melted.
3. In a large bowl, whisk together the melted coconut oil, maple syrup, cinnamon and salt. Stir in the oats, seeds and nuts.
4. Transfer the mixture to the lined baking tray and spread evenly.
5. Bake for 15 minutes. Remove from the oven, stir, spread the mixture out again and return to the oven to bake for a further 15 minutes until golden.
6. Leave the granola to cool, then transfer to an airtight jar. The granola will keep for a month.
7. *For the mango compote:* put all of the ingredients in a food processor and blitz until smooth. Store in an airtight container. The compote will keep for 2 weeks in the fridge.
8. *To serve:* load each bowl with 80g of granola, 80g of yogurt and 30g of compote. Add the blackberries and sliced banana, then sprinkle with coconut flakes, flaked almonds and chia seeds.

CHEF'S TIP: 'RUSTLE UP A BATCH OF THIS GRANOLA ON YOUR DAY OFF AND STORE IN A GLASS JAR – YOU'LL THANK YOURSELF WHEN YOU'RE IN A RUSH AND WANT A NUTRITIOUS BREAKFAST'

COFFEE PAIRING

Black americano

PLAYLIST PAIRING

Song: You're So Fine

Artist: Papa Bear & His Cubs

THE BOOKSHOP

Hereford, Herefordshire

This contemporary Hereford hangout is part of A Rule of Tum, a collection of indie restaurants established by a group of friends with a shared passion for quality food and caffeine.

The collective's first restaurant, Burger Shop, was a runaway success so, when the bookshop next door became available, the team jumped at the opportunity to transform it into their second casual dining spot. Homage is paid to the store's history via a floor-to-ceiling bookcase in the heart of the restaurant, while exposed brickwork, a concrete bar and leather banquettes add to the old-meets-new vibe.

The Bookshop has gained an enviable reputation for its award-winning Sunday lunches, steak nights and banging brunches – all of which are supplemented by stellar speciality-grade coffee.

RECIPE
SWEET POTATO HASH

SWEET POTATO HASH

Recipe by Callum McDonald of The Bookshop

Serves **2**
Preparation time **10 minutes**
Cooking time **20 minutes**

For the tahini dressing

Coriander 10g, chopped
Lemon ½, juice
Water 30ml
Tahini 30ml
Sugar a pinch
Salt a pinch

For the dukkah

Pumpkin seeds 2 tsp
Cumin seeds 1 tsp
Sesame seeds 2 tsp
Fennel seeds ½ tsp

For the hash

Sweet potatoes 2, peeled and diced into small cubes
Oil 10ml
Fennel seeds 2g
Cumin seeds 2g
Coriander seeds 2g
Onion 1, peeled and finely diced
Chickpeas 200g tin, drained
Spinach 60g
Spring onions 40g, finely sliced
Coriander 10g, roughly chopped

To serve

Free-range eggs 2, poached

1. *For the tahini dressing:* mix all of the ingredients together until smooth. Set aside.

2. *For the dukkah:* gently toast the seeds in a frying pan until fragrant. Set aside to cool.

3. *For the hash:* preheat the oven to 180°C / gas 4. Coat the potatoes in oil and roast for 10 minutes.

4. Toast the seeds in a frying pan until fragrant. Remove from the heat, place in a pestle and mortar and grind to a powder.

5. Using the same pan that was used for the spices, sweat the onions in a little oil until soft. Return the ground spices to the pan and add the chickpeas and roasted sweet potato. Stir until cooked through.

6. Add the spinach, spring onions and coriander to the pan, stirring until the spinach has wilted.

7. Serve the sweet potato hash with a poached egg, sprinkle of dukkah and drizzle of tahini dressing.

COFFEE PAIRING
Black americano

PLAYLIST PAIRING
Song: Fairground
Artist: Simply Red

CHEF'S TIP:
'CHOP THE DICED SWEET POTATOES EVENLY FOR A CONSISTENT ROAST'

BREAD & BUTTER

Truro, Cornwall

A haven in the heart of Truro, Bread & Butter is all about losing oneself in life's most delicious comforts. Breakfast sees brownies, muffins and frittatas sharing a morning menu with piles of American pancakes so light and fluffy you needn't worry about an eyes-bigger-than-stomach scenario. Pair your pick with a cup of Origin coffee – roasted in Porthleven – for the ultimate kick-starter.

By lunchtime, these breakfast staples give way to vibrant super-salads, soups and freshly made sourdough sandwiches. Ingredients are sourced locally where possible, including eggs from St Mawes, milk from Rodda's and bacon and ham from Kittow's.

RECIPE
VEGGIE FRITTATA

VEGGIE FRITTATA

Recipe by Kate Snell of Bread & Butter

Serves **6**
Preparation time **10 minutes**
Cooking time **35 minutes**

You will need

23 × 28cm baking tray

New potatoes a handful, chopped
Free-range eggs 12 large
Sea salt 1 tsp
Chipotle chilli flakes ½ tsp
Dried mixed herbs 1 tsp
Black pepper to season
Grated cheddar or crumbled feta 2 tbsp
Leek ¼, chopped
Spring onions 2, chopped
Cherry tomatoes a handful
Turmeric powder ¼ tsp
Any other vegetables ribboned courgettes, roasted red peppers, spinach (stalks removed)

1. Preheat the oven to 180°C / gas 4. Put the potatoes on a roasting tray, drizzle with olive oil and roast in the oven until lightly browned and cooked through.

2. Crack the eggs into a large bowl and whisk well.

3. Add the salt, chilli flakes, herbs and a few generous grinds of pepper. Mix well.

4. Add the roasted potatoes, cheese, leek, onions, tomatoes, turmeric and any extra vegetables. Gently stir to combine.

5. Line the baking tray with baking parchment then fill with the frittata mix.

6. Cook in the oven for 20 minutes, then rotate the tray and cook for another 10–15 minutes. Test the frittata with a cocktail stick to ensure it's cooked all the way through. Cut into slices and serve with crisp salad or homemade baked beans.

CHEF'S TIP: 'USE CORNISH SEA SALT'S SMOKED SALT FLAKES FOR AN UMAMI HIT'

COFFEE PAIRING

Origin Los Altos and Oatly flat white

PLAYLIST PAIRING

Song: Sunshine
Artist: Cleo Sol

WEAVER AND WILDE

Saddleworth, Greater Manchester

Visitors leave Weaver and Wilde grasping so much more than just a full takeaway cup. Not only does the speciality coffee shop serve quality brews and seasonal dishes, it's also a grocery and homewares emporium.

Farm-fresh veg, Saddleworth honey, bread from Roger's Bakery and milk from McLintock's Dairy are among the goodies that fight for shelf space with arty prints, houseplants and ceramics. Prepare for the inevitable and visit armed with a stash of empty Tupperware tubs and a clutch of tote bags.

RECIPE
CREAMY MUSHROOMS ON TOAST

CREAMY MUSHROOMS ON TOAST

Recipe by Cal Rowson-Codd of Weaver and Wilde

Serves **4–6**
Preparation time **30 minutes**
Cooking time **10 minutes**

Flat mushrooms 100g, roughly chopped

Portobello mushrooms 100g, roughly chopped

Chestnut mushrooms 100g, roughly chopped

Salt and pepper to season

Paprika ½ tbsp

Speciality mushrooms 100–150g

Fresh tarragon a small bunch, leaves picked

Double cream (or plant-based cream) 200–300ml

To serve

Lightly salted butter (or non-dairy spread)

Sourdough (or gluten-free alternative) 4–6 slices, toasted

Wild rocket to garnish

1. Place a wok or large pan over a medium-high heat. Add a splash of water and the mushrooms (except the speciality mushrooms). Season with a generous pinch of salt and pepper and sprinkle with the paprika. Cover the pan with a lid and give it a quick shake.

2. Cook, covered, for approximately 5 minutes, then add the speciality mushrooms and stir gently. The mushrooms should have released some moisture into the pan. If they haven't, add another splash of water. Cover and leave to cook for a further 5–10 minutes.

3. Remove the lid and gently stir the mushrooms. They should be not quite cooked (they retain heat well and will continue to cook on their own). Take off the heat, stir in the tarragon and leave to cool.

4. Drain the excess liquid from the mushrooms and set aside. Return the mushrooms to the heat. Add the double cream or plant-based cream (if using a plant-based cream, add some of the mushroom liquid to loosen further) and gently stir until simmering. Once the cream has started to reduce into a glossy sauce, take the pan off the heat.

5. Serve on buttered sourdough toast and garnish with a handful of wild rocket.

CHEF'S TIP: 'FOR ENHANCED FLAVOUR, COOK AND DRAIN THE MUSHROOMS A DAY IN ADVANCE AND STORE IN AN AIRTIGHT CONTAINER IN THE FRIDGE'

COFFEE PAIRING

Flat white

PLAYLIST PAIRING

Song: Change the Skyline
Artist: Duran Duran

SACRED GROUNDS

Exeter, Devon

Creative plant-based dishes, speciality-grade coffee and upbeat vibes make this day-to-night dining spot a crowd puller.

The seasonal all-day menus feature thrilling compilations, from brisket pulled jackfruit sandwiches topped with melted cheese, peppers, crispy onions and mustard to chai-spiced porridge with almond drizzle, cherry jam, strawberry and almond flakes.

Coffee is given the same care and attention as the freshly prepped dishes. Expertly bronzed beans from Devon's Roastworks Coffee Co. are paired with a range of alt milks to create a tempting line-up of espresso-based drinks.

Visit on Friday or Saturday evenings to enjoy small plates, cocktails and natural wines by candlelight at Sacred Nights.

RECIPE
SACRED SCRAMBLED TOFU

SACRED SCRAMBLED TOFU

Recipe by Sacred Grounds

Serves **3-4**
Preparation time **10 minutes**
Cooking time **20 minutes**

Vegetable oil 1 tbsp

Red onion 1, peeled and finely sliced

Sugar 1 tsp

Sea salt and black pepper a pinch

Smoked paprika 1 tsp

Turmeric ½ tsp

Firm tofu 400g pack, drained and patted dry

Garlic 2 cloves, peeled and finely chopped

Red chilli ½, finely diced

Parsley a handful, finely chopped

Cherry tomatoes 8, quartered

Spinach leaves a handful

To serve

Olive oil 1 tsp

Sourdough 6 slices, toasted

Large avocados 2, peeled, pitted and sliced

Sumac to season

Pea shoots to garnish

1. Heat the cooking oil in a large frying pan over a medium heat. Add the onion and gently sauté until soft.
2. Put the sugar, salt and pepper, smoked paprika, turmeric and tofu in a bowl. Using your hands, gently crumble the tofu and mix with the other ingredients.
3. Add the garlic and chilli to the frying pan and cook for a few minutes, stirring so the garlic doesn't burn.
4. Add the seasoned tofu to the pan and cook for 5-6 minutes until the tofu is cooked through.
5. Remove the pan from the heat and stir in the parsley, tomatoes and spinach until the spinach wilts. Season to taste.
6. *To assemble:* drizzle the olive oil over the toasted sourdough, then top with scrambled tofu. Place some sliced avocado to the side and sprinkle with sumac. Garnish with pea shoots and finish with a drizzle of olive oil and sprinkle of salt and pepper.

CHEF'S TIP: 'ADD BEANS AND AUBERGINE BACON FOR A PLANT-POWERED BRUNCH'

COFFEE PAIRING

Roastworks The Truth oat-milk flat white

PLAYLIST PAIRING

Song: Waxahatchee
Artist: Lilacs

TINCAN COFFEE CO
Bristol

Tincan's eco-centric North Street cafe has garnered a sterling reputation for top-notch coffee and award-winning brunch dishes.

Clued-up baristas sling consistently good espresso and fashion clean-as-a-whistle filters using beans roasted by Clifton Coffee, plus a bevy of small-batch roasteries. And while the coffee crew brew up a storm behind the bar, in the kitchen chef André Davies creates crowd-pleasing dishes from local ingredients.

In line with the cafe's ethical stance, the vibrant food menu changes with the seasons. Dishes such as poached eggs with pea guacamole, chimichurri and chilli sit alongside cheese toasties, stuffed pastries and breakfast-bun staples. The food is so good that Tincan even picked up a Best Cafe Food gong in the Bristol Good Food Awards.

RECIPE
TIRAMISU FRENCH TOAST

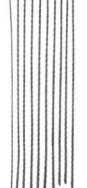

Tiramisu French Toast

Recipe by André Davies of Tincan Coffee Co

Serves **6**
Preparation time **10 minutes**
Cooking time **6 minutes**

For the coffee glaze

Espresso 100ml

Maple syrup 100ml

Salt a pinch

For the custard

Espresso 1 double shot

Free-range eggs 3 large

Free-range egg yolks 2

Cocoa powder ½ tsp

Salt ½ tsp

Light soft brown sugar 23g

Double cream 120ml

Milk 180ml

For the mascarpone cream

Mascarpone 250g

Double cream 250ml

Caster sugar 60g

To assemble

Butter 20g

Brioche 1 large loaf, cut into 2½cm slices

Pistachios 50g, shelled and crushed

Orange 1, zest

1. *For the coffee glaze:* put all of the ingredients in a saucepan over a medium heat. Bring to the boil, then reduce the temperature and simmer for 5 minutes until a syrup forms. Set aside and leave to cool.

2. *For the custard:* put all of the ingredients, except for the cream and milk, in a large bowl. Whisk together until smooth, then slowly add the cream and milk, whisking continuously. Set aside.

3. *For the mascarpone cream:* put all of the ingredients in a large bowl and whisk together until it's thick and can hold a firm peak. Refrigerate.

4. *To assemble:* heat a large non-stick frying pan over a medium heat. Add the butter and slowly melt until foaming. Dip the brioche into the custard for 30 seconds on each side then carefully place in the pan. Cook for 3 minutes on each side until golden brown and the custard has set throughout the brioche.

5. Drizzle some of the coffee glaze onto a plate, scatter with a pinch of pistachios, then place a slice of cooked brioche in the centre. Top with a big scoop of mascarpone cream, another sprinkle of pistachios and a drizzle of coffee glaze. Garnish with orange zest.

CHEF'S TIP: 'SWAP THE PISTACHIOS FOR WALNUTS AND SLICED BANANA TO TURN THIS INTO A BREAKFAST TREAT'

COFFEE PAIRING

Tincan's House Blend cappuccino

PLAYLIST PAIRING

Song: Figure of 8
Artist: Two Day Coma

WAYLAND'S YARD

Birmingham, Bristol and Worcester

All-day brunching is the big draw at the Wayland's Yard trio of speciality cafes. Whether you visit the Worcester, Birmingham or Bristol branch, you'll discover a contemporary space in which to drink good coffee, meet friends and chow down on delicious food.

Hero dishes on the WY menus include chorizo and halloumi skillet-pan hash, veggie brunch baps stuffed with homemade hash browns, avo, halloumi and chilli jam, and raspberry pancakes drizzled with greek yogurt, raspberry coulis and a white choc, almond and sesame crumb.

Coffee beans are bronzed by the house roastery (under the moniker Odd Kin Coffee Roasters) in Bristol, while an ever-changing line-up of guests from the team's favourite roasteries also features.

RECIPE

EGGY CRUMPETS WITH CHILLI JAM AND HALLOUMI

EGGY CRUMPETS WITH CHILLI JAM AND HALLOUMI

Recipe by Charlie Ingle of Wayland's Yard

Serves **5**
Preparation time **10 minutes**
Cooking time **1 hour for chilli jam, 10 minutes for crumpets**

For the chilli jam

Red peppers 3, deseeded and roughly chopped

Large red chillies 2, deseeded and roughly chopped

Light brown soft sugar 60g

Apple cider vinegar 225ml

Smoked paprika ¾ tsp

For the eggy crumpets

Free-range eggs 6

Milk 55ml

Chilli flakes ½ tsp

Dried thyme 1 tsp

Salt and pepper to taste

Cooking oil ⅔ tbsp

Crumpets 10

To serve

Halloumi 400g, sliced diagonally into triangles

Chives small bunch, finely sliced

Spring onions small bunch, finely sliced

Red chillies 2, finely sliced

1. *For the chilli jam:* put all of the ingredients in a deep saucepan over a medium heat, mix well and bring to a simmer. Stir occasionally, and cook until the peppers and chillies are soft and have started to darken. You'll know it's ready when the mixture continues to bubble for around 30 seconds when the pan is removed from the heat.

2. Leave the chilli jam to cool for 10 minutes then, while still warm, blend using a stick blender or food processor. Blitz until it's reached the desired consistency – it can be as smooth or chunky as you like.

3. Once the jam has cooled completely, pour it into a jar or tub and store in the fridge. It will keep for a week.

4. *For the eggy crumpets:* crack the eggs into a large bowl. Whisk in the milk, chilli flakes, dried thyme and salt and pepper until combined.

5. Pour a drizzle of oil into a large frying pan and place over a medium-high heat. Rotate the pan to spread the oil evenly.

6. One at a time, submerge the crumpets in the egg mixture, ensuring they are fully saturated.

7. Transfer the crumpets from the bowl to the pan, placing them hole-side-down. Push them down using the back of a spatula and reduce the heat to medium. Leave them to cook for 2-3 minutes or until they are golden brown, then flip over and repeat on the other side. Give them a final squeeze with the spatula to ensure they're cooked through – if any egg oozes out, turn down the heat and cook for a further minute on each side.

8. *To serve:* while the crumpets are cooking, place a drizzle of oil in a separate pan over a medium heat. Once hot, add the halloumi and cook until golden brown on each side. Set aside.

9. Place a large tbsp of chilli jam in the centre of each plate and spread it with the back of the spoon. Place 2 crumpets on top, then the halloumi and finish with a sprinkle of chives, spring onion and chilli.

CHEF'S TIP: 'IF THE JAM IS TOO THICK WHEN COOLED, ADD A LITTLE BOILING WATER AND MIX. IF IT'S TOO THIN, POP IT BACK ON A MEDIUM HEAT FOR A WHILE LONGER, STIRRING CONTINUOUSLY'

COFFEE PAIRING

Filter

PLAYLIST PAIRING

Song: Brothers on the Slide
Artist: Cymande

LAYNES

Leeds, Yorkshire

For over a decade, Laynes has been the first stop on any coffee fan's tour of the caffeine-rich city of Leeds. The pioneering coffee shop is located a 30-second dash from Leeds train station so, since it opened in 2011, it's enjoyed an almost constant stream of commuters dropping in for their daily espresso hit.

While Laynes' enviable reputation was initially built on its pioneering use of speciality coffee, the past few years have seen the team earn equal kudos for their brunch offering. The same attention to detail and consistency that goes into every flat white is applied to dishes such as kale and spring onion bubble and squeak with fried eggs and roasted tomatoes, and fritters with spiced kasundi.

RECIPE

SMOKED HADDOCK POTATO CAKES WITH KALE PESTO AND POACHED EGGS

SMOKED HADDOCK POTATO CAKES WITH KALE PESTO AND POACHED EGGS

Recipe by James Palmer of Laynes

Serves **4**
Preparation time **15 minutes**
Cooking time **20 minutes**

For the kale pesto

Kale 250g, stems removed
Basil leaves 50g
Parsley 50g
Parmesan 50g, finely grated
Pine nuts 100g
Garlic 2 cloves, peeled
Olive oil 4 tbsp

For the smoked haddock potato cakes

Whole milk 570ml
Smoked haddock fillets 4
Large potatoes 2, peeled and chopped into quarters
Butter 50g
Salt and pepper to taste
Olive oil 2 tbsp
Leek 1, a quarter of the leek cut into 1cm slices, the rest thinly sliced
Garlic 2 cloves, peeled and minced
Chives 25g, finely chopped

For the poached eggs

White wine vinegar 3 tbsp
Free-range eggs 4

To garnish

Watercress 100g
Crème fraîche 200g
Sumac 10g
Lemon 1, halved

1. *For the pesto:* put all of the ingredients in a food processor and blitz until smooth. Set aside.

2. *For the potato cakes:* preheat the oven to 180°C / gas 4. Pour the milk into a saucepan and bring to a simmer. Poach the smoked haddock fillets in the milk until just cooked. Remove the haddock from the milk and allow to cool (the fish will keep cooking for a little while, so it's important to remove from the heat before it's fully cooked).

3. Bring a saucepan of salted water to the boil, add the potatoes and cook until tender. Drain the potatoes then return them to the pan. Add the butter and mash together until smooth. Season to taste and set aside.

4. Place 1 tbsp of olive oil in a frying pan over a medium heat. Add the 1cm leek slices and minced garlic. Once the leeks and garlic start to brown, set aside and leave to cool.

5. Add another tbsp of olive oil to the pan and char the thinly sliced leek. Remove from the pan and set aside.

6. *To assemble the potato cakes:* flake the cooked haddock into the mashed potato. Add the 1cm cooked leeks (saving the finely chopped leeks for later) and chives to the pan and combine. Take ¼ of the mixture and mould into a patty approximately 2cm thick. Repeat for the other 3 potato cakes.

7. Add a splash of olive oil to a hot frying pan and sear the cakes on both sides until lightly browned, then finish in the oven for 10 minutes.

8. *For the poached eggs:* while the cakes are cooking in the oven, bring a pan of water to the boil. Add the white wine vinegar then turn down the heat until the water is at a simmer. Crack an egg into the water and cook for 3 minutes until poached. Repeat for the remaining eggs.

9. *To serve:* drizzle 2 tbsp of the kale pesto onto each plate, then place the potato cakes on top. Top each cake with a poached egg and garnish with watercress, a tbsp of crème fraîche and the thinly sliced leek. Finish with a sprinkle of sumac and a squeeze of lemon juice.

CHEF'S TIP: 'TO PREVENT THE YOLKS FROM SETTING DURING POACHING, CRACK THE EGG AS CLOSE AS POSSIBLE TO THE WATER'S SURFACE. ONCE COOKED, CHECK HOW FIRM IT IS BY GIVING IT A GENTLE PRESS ON A SOLID SURFACE – IT SHOULD BOUNCE BACK'

COFFEE PAIRING

Square Mile Coffee Roasters El Eucalipto Peru filter

PLAYLIST PAIRING

Song: Fillet-O-Rapper

Artist: MF Doom

PAPERCUP COFFEE

Glasgow

At this community-focused cafe on Glasgow's Great Western Road, a skilled and upbeat team of baristas serves a menu of exquisite coffees roasted just a stone's throw away at Papercup's roastery HQ.

At the brew bar, high-scoring beans are fashioned into beautiful espresso and filter drinks, each one crafted with care. The same attention to detail is applied by the creative kitchen team who use ethical and sustainable ingredients in their line-up of tempting brunch and lunch dishes.

Coffee aficionados can enjoy further Papercup thrills by visiting its industrial-style roastery and watching the roasting magic happen while they sip a brew made from the latest batch.

RECIPE

THAI YELLOW EGGS WITH MANGO CHUTNEY AND SALTED CUCUMBER

THAI YELLOW EGGS WITH MANGO CHUTNEY AND SALTED CUCUMBER

Recipe by Graeme Crawford of Papercup Coffee

Serves **2**
Preparation time **20 minutes**
Cooking time **30 minutes**

For the salted cucumber

Cucumber ¼, deseeded and sliced diagonally into 5mm pieces
Salt 1 tsp

For the curry

Vegetable oil
Yellow curry paste (we use Mae Ploy) 1 tbsp
Onion 1, peeled and diced
Potato 1, peeled and diced
Red lentils 50g
Coconut milk 400ml
Palm sugar thumb-size piece, crushed
Light soy sauce 1 tbsp

For the eggs

Free-range eggs 4, beaten
Butter 1 knob

To serve

Paratha bread 1
Mango chutney 1 tsp
Roasted coconut chips 1 tsp
Crispy onions 1 tsp
Coriander 1 tbsp, chopped
Lime ½, zest

1. *For the salted cucumber:* put the cucumber in a bowl and massage with salt. Leave to ferment at room temperature until ready to use.

2. *For the curry:* heat a glug of oil in a large saucepan over a low heat and fry the curry paste until fragrant. Add the onion and cook until soft – if the paste starts to burn, loosen with a splash of coconut milk.

3. Add the potatoes and coat in the paste, then add the lentils, followed by the coconut milk. Cook for around 20 minutes, stirring occasionally, until the lentils and potato are al dente. If the sauce becomes too thick, loosen with a splash of water – although it should be a thick curry.

4. Add the palm sugar and cook until melted, then season with the soy sauce. Taste and adjust seasoning if required.

5. Heat the paratha in a hot pan, flipping it when it starts to char. Remove from the pan when cooked on both sides and set aside.

6. *For the eggs:* heat the butter in a pan over a medium heat and, once melted, add the eggs and whip into scrambled eggs. Season with salt and pepper.

7. *To serve:* place 2 ladles of curry in each shallow bowl. Heap the scrambled eggs on top and garnish with the salted cucumber, mango chutney, coconut chips and crispy onions. Sprinkle with coriander and freshly grated lime zest and serve with the paratha.

CHEF'S TIP: 'THIS DISH PROVIDES THE PERFECT BALANCE OF SWEET, SOUR, SALT AND SPICE – BUT YOU CAN RAMP UP THE HEAT FURTHER WITH A TOUCH OF SRIRACHA WHEN PLATING'

COFFEE PAIRING
Cold brew

PLAYLIST PAIRING
Song: Even After All
Artist: Finley Quaye

BREAKFAST & BRUNCH

LAY OF THE LAND

Settle, Yorkshire

Speciality beans and splendid blooms might be an unusual duo of delights, but this bijou garden centre in Settle happily combines the two. After wandering the aisles lusting over the beautiful flora, visitors can pop into the cafe to sample Casa Espresso coffee served as espresso, AeroPress or pourover.

There's always something new to sip in this freshly refurbished space: beans get switched up every few weeks to reflect seasonal harvests, while a decent selection of loose-leaf teas delivers quality cuppas.

It's not just plants and coffee that are well tended at this family-run set-up. Youngest son James 'Jimmie' Lay, who trained at Michelin-starred Northcote in Langho, sees to it that pretty much everything is homemade using kitchen-garden and locally supplied produce.

RECIPE

CRUMPETS WITH SLOW-COOKED PORTOBELLO MUSHROOMS, BEETROOT RELISH AND ROCKET PESTO

CRUMPETS WITH SLOW-COOKED PORTOBELLO MUSHROOMS, BEETROOT RELISH AND ROCKET PESTO

Recipe by James Lay of Lay of the Land

Serves **4**
Preparation time **30 minutes (plus proving time)**
Cooking time **40 minutes**

You will need

9–10cm crumpet rings (egg rings work too)

For the crumpets (makes 10)

Milk 240ml
Strong white flour 250g
Fresh yeast 14g
Sea salt 1 tsp
Sugar ½ tsp
Bicarbonate of soda ½ tsp

For the slow-cooked mushrooms

Portobello mushrooms 4
Garlic 2 cloves, peeled and chopped
Rosemary 1 sprig, chopped
Salt and pepper a pinch
Rapeseed oil 3 tsp

For the beetroot relish

Golden granulated sugar 250g
White wine vinegar 250ml
Raw beetroot 600g, peeled and grated
Garlic 2 cloves, crushed
Cumin seeds 1 tsp
Fennel seeds 1 tsp

For the rocket pesto

Rocket 150g
Pine nuts 50g
Lemon juice ½ tsp
Rapeseed oil 150g

1. *For the crumpets:* gently heat the milk in a saucepan until it's lukewarm. Put the remaining ingredients in a mixing bowl and slowly stir in the warm milk to make a smooth batter, being careful not to overmix. Cover the bowl with a clean tea towel and set aside somewhere warm to prove for 40 minutes.

2. *For the slow-cooked mushrooms:* preheat the oven to 160°C / gas 3. Combine all of the ingredients in a ovenproof dish, cover with foil and cook in the oven for approximately 40 minutes.

3. *For the beetroot relish:* in a saucepan over a medium heat, dissolve the sugar in the vinegar. Once the sugar has dissolved, add the rest of the ingredients and continue to cook until the liquid has thickened slightly and the beetroot is cooked. This should take 30–40 minutes.

4. *For the rocket pesto:* put all the ingredients in a blender and blitz until smooth. Season with salt and pepper to taste.

5. *For the crumpets:* melt a knob of butter in a heavy-based non-stick pan over a medium heat. Place as many crumpet rings as will fit in the pan, then pour approximately 3 tbsp of batter into each. Cook until the bubbles in the top begin to pop and the mixture starts to set. Remove the rings carefully (use a tea towel – they will be hot), then flip the crumpets and cook for a further 2 minutes.

6. *To assemble:* place a buttered crumpet in the centre of each plate, top with beetroot relish and 1 slow-cooked portobello mushroom. Drizzle with rocket pesto, then season with salt and pepper and serve.

CHEF'S TIP: 'ANY LEFTOVER COOKED CRUMPETS WILL KEEP IN THE FRIDGE FOR UP TO FOUR DAYS, SO YOU CAN ENJOY THEM FOR BREAKFAST ANOTHER TIME'

COFFEE PAIRING

Casa Espresso Brazil
Patricia flat white

PLAYLIST PAIRING

Song: Crooked Teeth
Artist: Death Cab for Cutie

BREAKFAST & BRUNCH

WHIPPED RICOTTA ON SOURDOUGH WITH OLIVE, BASIL AND SUN-DRIED TOMATO TAPENADE

LUNCH & SUPPER

COURGETTE AND PEPPER FRITTERS WITH BEETROOT AND APPLE SLAW	94
GLASRACH PIZZA	98
ROASTED BROCCOLI WITH TAHINI AND CRANBERRIES	102
WHIPPED RICOTTA ON SOURDOUGH WITH OLIVE, BASIL AND SUN-DRIED TOMATO TAPENADE	106
KIMCHINI	110
LAMB SHAWARMA WITH CORIANDER FLATBREADS	114
BUTTERNUT SQUASH DAL WITH CRUNCHY SPICED CHICKPEAS	118
COFFEE-GLAZED BARBECUE SHORT RIBS AND SLAW	122

ARCHIVE

Leeds, Yorkshire

The actors and production teams who create TV programmes and indie films at Leeds' Prime Studios don't have to settle for second rate catering-style coffee thanks to this on-site cafe bar.

Housed in a former ITV archive, the speciality coffee spot is also open to the public who swing by for morning brews, lunch and post-work drinks. Casa Espresso supplies the A-list house beans for the main grinder, although other red-carpet roasteries make guest appearances throughout the year.

Between takes, stars join regular punters to chow down on appetising brunch and lunch dishes from a small but perfectly formed menu.

RECIPE
COURGETTE AND PEPPER FRITTERS WITH BEETROOT AND APPLE SLAW

COURGETTE AND PEPPER FRITTERS WITH BEETROOT AND APPLE SLAW

Recipe by Matt Griffiths of Archive

Serves **4**
Preparation time **45 minutes**
Cooking time **10–15 minutes**

For the beetroot and apple slaw

Green apple 1, peeled and grated

Beetroot 3, cooked, peeled and grated

Fresh chilli 1 tbsp, chopped

Salt and pepper a pinch

For the courgette and pepper fritters

Smoked paprika 1 tbsp

Free-range eggs 2 large, lightly beaten

Plain flour 2 tbsp

Sea salt and pepper a pinch

Red peppers 2, deseeded and thinly sliced

Red onion 1, peeled and thinly sliced

Courgettes 2, grated

Plain flour

To serve

Free-range eggs 4, fried

Chilli jam 100g

Walnuts 100g, chopped

Goat's cheese 150g

Vegetable oil 4 tbsp

Optional garnishes

Chives finely chopped

Flat-leaf parsley chopped

1. *For the beetroot and apple slaw:* put all of the ingredients in a large mixing bowl, combine and set aside.

2. *For the courgette and pepper fritters:* put the paprika, eggs, flour, salt and black pepper in a large bowl. Mix well until it becomes a smooth batter, then add the pepper, onion and courgette.

3. In another large mixing bowl, combine a handful of flour with $\frac{1}{8}$ of the fritter mixture. Shape into a round ball roughly the size of a satsuma. Repeat until you have 8 fritters.

4. Warm 2 tbsp of vegetable oil in a medium-size pan over a medium heat. Once the oil is hot, place the fritters in the pan and press down using the back of a metal spatula. Cook until golden brown then flip to cook the other side.

5. *To serve:* place 2 tbsps of chilli jam in the centre of each plate and use a spoon to spread into a circle. Place 2 fritters on top of the jam, followed by a fried egg. Add the slaw to one side of the fritter stack, then sprinkle with the walnuts and goat's cheese. Garnish with chives and/or parsley.

CHEF'S TIP: 'ADD A TEASPOON OF HARISSA PASTE TO THE FRITTER MIX FOR EXTRA KICK'

COFFEE PAIRING

Archive Espresso Blend long black

PLAYLIST PAIRING

Song: Dance
Artist: ESG

CAFE SIA

Broadford, Isle of Skye

Why travel to Naples for syrupy own-roasted espresso and Italian-style pizza when you can find them on the beautiful Isle of Skye?

After co-managing a Michelin-starred hotel on the island for several years, Tom Eveling decided to leave hotel life and drive all the way to Pisa to pick up a wood-fired oven. His plan was to open a cafe on Skye and share his passion for authentic pizza, speciality coffee and wine with the island's visitors and locals.

The result of this epic trip is the popular Cafe Sia, a much-loved meeting place which blends Scottish and Mediterranean influences in everything from its pizza toppings to its whisky coffee chasers.

RECIPE
GLASRACH PIZZA

GLASRACH PIZZA

Recipe by Cafe Sia

Makes **4 pizzas**
Preparation time **60-90 minutes**
Cooking time **15 minutes**

For the dough

Dried yeast 1 dsp

Salt 1 tsp

Caster sugar 1 tsp

Olive oil 100ml

Water 600ml at approx 37°C

Strong bread flour (pizza flour or gluten-free flour also work) 1kg

For the sauce

Tomato paste 200g

Chopped tomatoes 400g tin

Garlic cloves 2, peeled and crushed

Italian seasoning 1 tsp

Caster sugar 1 tsp

Salt and black pepper a pinch

For the garlic oil

Garlic 1 bulb, peeled

Olive oil 175ml

For the toppings

Red peppers 3, deseeded and sliced

Artichoke hearts 3-4, chopped

Mushrooms 6-8, chopped

Sun-dried tomatoes 16-20

Leeks 1-2, sliced

Green and black olives 20-24, pitted and chopped

Mozzarella or vegan cheese 400g, grated

1. *For the dough:* put the yeast, salt, sugar, oil and water in a mixer with a hook attachment. Turn on and slowly add the flour until all the flour is used and a soft dough formed. Remove the dough from the mixer and knead lightly on a floured surface for approximately 5 minutes. Put the dough in a bowl, cover with clingfilm and leave it somewhere warm for around 1 hour until doubled in size.

2. *For the sauce:* put all of the ingredients in a blender and blitz until smooth.

3. *For the garlic oil:* put all of the ingredients in a blender and blitz until smooth.

4. *For the topping:* preheat the oven to 180°C / gas 4. Put the sliced red peppers on an oven tray, drizzle with olive oil, season with salt and pepper, then roast in the oven for 5 minutes.

5. Turn the oven up to 200°C / gas 6. Split the dough into 4 balls and roll out to form 4 circular pizza bases. Place the bases on pre-oiled trays, working the dough to the edges. Cook for 5 minutes, then turn over and cook for another 5 minutes.

6. Remove the bases from the oven and spread a couple of tablespoons of the sauce on top of each. Top with your choice of the toppings, finishing with the cheese. Cook for a further 5 minutes, keeping a close eye to make sure they don't burn.

CHEF'S TIP: 'GLASRACH IS GAELIC FOR 'VEGETARIAN'. HOWEVER, IF YOU WANT TO ADD MEAT, A FEW SLICES OF PROSCIUTTO WORK WELL'

COFFEE PAIRING

Coffee shake – double shot espresso with milk and ice cream

PLAYLIST PAIRING

Song: Abracadabra

Artist: Steve Miller Band

FOODSTORY

Aberdeen

This Thistle Street cafe is at the forefront of both sustainable dining and top-drawer speciality coffee.

Locals and visitors swing by to sip exceptional brews – roasted by the likes of Dear Green and Obadiah – and feast on award-winning casual dishes. The exclusively veggie menu includes lots of punchy salads and chilli bowls which are served in a buzzy setting.

Aberdeen beach bums, meanwhile, head to sister venue Foodstory Beach Hut Bakery on the esplanade, where plant-based pastries, glazed buns, sourdough toasties and glorious coffee are served out of a refurbished food truck.

RECIPE
ROASTED BROCCOLI WITH TAHINI AND CRANBERRIES

ROASTED BROCCOLI WITH TAHINI AND CRANBERRIES

Recipe by Sandy McKinnon of Foodstory

Serves **2 as a main or 4 as a side**
Preparation time **10 minutes**
Cooking time **15 minutes**

Broccoli 2, florets chopped into bite-size pieces and stalks finely chopped

Tenderstem broccoli a handful

Oil

Chopped almonds 50g

Kale 100g

Cranberries 50g

For the dressing

Tahini 200ml

Garlic 2 cloves, peeled and finely chopped

Lemon juice 50ml

Sunflower oil 45ml

Olive oil 140ml

Salt and pepper a generous pinch

1. Preheat the oven to 210°C / gas 8. Put the broccoli florets, stalks and Tenderstem on a baking tray, season with salt and pepper and drizzle with oil. Roast for 10–15 minutes until slightly crisp. Set aside to cool.

2. On a separate oven tray, roast the almonds for 4 minutes until lightly toasted.

3. Blanch the kale in boiling water, then plunge into cold water and leave for 5 minutes. Drain in a colander and set aside.

4. *For the dressing:* put the tahini, garlic, lemon juice, sunflower oil and olive oil in a bowl. Using a hand blender, blitz the mixture until smooth and creamy. Add more olive oil if it's too thick to drizzle. Season to taste and set aside.

5. Put the cooled broccoli (leaving out the Tenderstem), cooled almonds, blanched kale and cranberries in a mixing bowl. Stir in ⅔ of the dressing.

6. Transfer the mix into a serving bowl. Top with the Tenderstem and drizzle with the remaining dressing.

CHEF'S TIP: 'MAKE EXTRA DRESSING AND KEEP IT IN THE FRIDGE AS A DELICIOUS DIP FOR OTHER VEGGIES'

COFFEE PAIRING

Espresso tonic with a slice of orange

PLAYLIST PAIRING

Song: Véia

Artist: Seu Jorge

LUNCH & SUPPER

TOAST HOUSE

Ikley, Yorkshire

The team at Toast House are unashamedly devoted to toast and celebrate it in all its golden glory. Slowly proved sourdough is the humble foundation on which Toast's innovative homemade masterpieces are crafted.

Appropriately, the light and airy venue feels delightfully homely and chatter floats freely between bakers and diners. Freshly baked cakes capture visitors' attention while shelves, sideboards and tables are bedecked with homewares and artisan foods waiting to be bought and taken home.

The crew take the art of coffee as seriously as the craft of baking and have collaborated with respected Leeds roastery North Star in the development of their bespoke espresso blend.

RECIPE

WHIPPED RICOTTA ON SOURDOUGH WITH OLIVE, BASIL AND SUN-DRIED TOMATO TAPENADE

Whipped Ricotta on Sourdough with Olive, Basil and Sun-dried Tomato Tapenade

Recipe by Natasha Byers and Lisa Jenkins of Toast House

Serves **4**
Preparation time **20 minutes**
Cooking time **5 minutes**

For the whipped ricotta

Ricotta 250g

Full-fat cream cheese 200g

Lemon ½, zest

Garlic granules a pinch

White wine vinegar ½ tsp

Sea salt and black pepper to season

For the tapenade

Pitted green olives 180g, drained

Pitted black olives 90g, drained

Sun-dried tomatoes 140g, drained and roughly chopped

Fresh basil 10g, roughly chopped

Garlic clove 1, grated

Lemon 1, zest and juice

Olive oil

Freshly ground black pepper to taste

To serve

Sourdough toasted

Salted butter

Basil leaves to garnish

1. *For the whipped ricotta:* put the ricotta, cream cheese, lemon zest, garlic granules and white wine vinegar in a bowl and combine gently with a fork. Season to taste and set aside.

2. *For the tapenade:* put all of the tapenade ingredients (except the olive oil and black pepper) in a food processor. Blitz briefly then add 1 tbsp of oil and repeat the process until you have the desired texture. Season to taste with black pepper – you won't need to add salt as the olives and sun-dried tomatoes are salty.

3. *To serve:* toast the sourdough until golden then spread with salted butter. Top with the whipped ricotta and a dollop of tapenade, then garnish with basil leaves and a drizzle of olive oil.

CHEFS' TIP: 'ADD FRESH HERBS TO THE RICOTTA AND SERVE WITH TOASTED WALNUTS OR PINE NUTS'

COFFEE PAIRING
Iced americano

PLAYLIST PAIRING
Song: I Think I'll Call It Morning
Artist: Gil Scott-Heron

LUNCH & SUPPER

BLOCK

Barnstaple, Devon

For excellent coffee and contemporary street food, you'd be hard pressed to beat this slice of urban cool sandwiched among the indie stores and cafes of Barnstaple's Butchers Row.

The ever-changing menu is a globetrotting affair. At breakfast, huevos rancheros and sky-high American-style pancakes rub shoulders with bacon butties, then, come lunch, a line-up of fresh and healthy midday dishes takes inspiration from the East. Hard-to-fake favourites like ramen, pho and katsu curry are crafted with authenticity and care.

Fantastic food is only half the story as you'd be mad to miss out on a glossy Origin Coffee flat white served in a vintage pottery cup. Sip at your leisure while enjoying Block's lively bustle.

RECIPE
KIMCHINI

KIMCHINI

Recipe by Andy Stephenson of Block

Serves **4 as a starter/lunch**
Preparation time **15 minutes**
Cooking time **15–30 minutes**

Sushi rice (short-grain rice also works) 250g

Kimchi 125g

Plain flour 100g, seasoned with a pinch of salt and pepper

Free-range eggs 2, lightly beaten

Panko breadcrumbs 100g

Gochujang 1 tbsp

Soy sauce 1 tbsp

Sriracha mayonnaise (mix 1 tbsp of mayo with a squeeze of sriracha)

Chilli sauce (we use Lao Gan Ma Chilli Crisp) 3 tsp

Chives a pinch, chopped

1. Wash the rice thoroughly (until the water runs clear), then cook as per packet instructions. If using a rice cooker, use a 1:1 rice-to-water ratio.

2. Pulse the kimchi in a blender until the pieces are roughly the same size as the cooked rice grains, but still retain some texture.

3. When the rice is cooked, put it in a mixing bowl with the kimchi, gochujang and soy sauce and combine. Sample the mixture and season to taste – if you think it needs more salt, add either a pinch of salt or a splash of soy sauce.

4. When the rice is cool enough to handle, roll into golf-ball-size balls (15–20) and set aside on a baking tray.

5. Set up a small breading station by placing the flour, beaten eggs and panko breadcrumbs on three separate dinner plates.

6. One at a time, roll the rice balls in the flour, then the egg and finally the breadcrumbs. Set aside on a baking tray.

7. **To cook the kimchini:** either shallow fry the balls in small batches, deep fry them at 180°C for 3–5 minutes or bake in the oven for 10–20 minutes at 180°C / gas 4 until crisp and golden.

8. **To serve:** place a few dollops of sriracha mayo on each plate and place a kimchini on top of each. Crown with chilli sauce and a sprinkling of chopped chives.

CHEF'S TIP: 'THIS RECIPE WORKS BEST WITH FRESHLY COOKED RICE AS IT'S MORE MALLEABLE'

COFFEE PAIRING

Espresso Martini

PLAYLIST PAIRING

Song: Lover
Artist: Mioko Yamaguchi

THE CARTSHED

Wallingford, Oxfordshire

Head to this listed barn on an Oxfordshire farm for a flat white in gorgeous rural surroundings. Its friendly and open vibe is complemented by an exposed-beam ceiling and floor-to-ceiling windows, while red brick walls and wooden floors and furniture add rustic charm.

The cafe, which is on the banks of the River Thames, attracts walkers and families, so expect to find all generations tucking into hearty breakfasts, delicious brunches and afternoon teas. Check out the ever-evolving specials board if you fancy an out-of-the-ordinary lunch.

The Cartshed team are passionate about local produce and use wheat from the farm in the creation of their sourdough loaves. Coffee is sourced from Dark Horse Roastery, three miles down the road.

RECIPE

LAMB SHAWARMA WITH CORIANDER FLATBREADS

LAMB SHAWARMA WITH CORIANDER FLATBREADS

Recipe by Callum Bell of The Cartshed

Serves **6–8**
Preparation time **5 minutes (plus 4 hours marinating)**
Cooking time **4 hours**

For the lamb

Sumac ¼ tsp
Ground nutmeg ¼ tsp
Ground allspice ¼ tsp
Ras el hanout ¼ tsp
Ground cumin ¼ tsp
Ground coriander ¼ tsp
Dried oregano ¼ tsp
Garlic 1 clove, peeled and sliced
Onion 1, peeled and sliced
Sunflower oil 50ml
Lamb shoulder 750g, diced

For the flatbreads

Plain flour 100g
Baking powder a pinch
Salt and pepper a pinch
Garlic 1 clove, minced
Fresh coriander a handful, chopped
Warm water 50ml
Vegetable or sunflower oil 1 tbsp (more as needed)

To serve

Greek yogurt
Fresh coriander
Pickled radish (see page 118 for recipe)
Herby couscous salad
Roasted beetroot hummus

1. *For the lamb:* prepare the marinade by combining the spices and herbs with the garlic, onion and sunflower oil in a large bowl.

2. Put the lamb in the bowl and coat in the marinade. Cover the bowl, place in the fridge and leave to marinate for at least 4 hours or overnight.

3. Preheat the oven to 150°C / gas 2.

4. In a frying pan, fry the lamb in batches to sear the edges. Put in a roasting tin, cover with foil and place in the oven to braise in its juices for 3 hours.

5. *For the coriander and garlic flatbreads:* in a large bowl, mix the flour, baking powder, salt, pepper, garlic and coriander.

6. Make a well in the centre, then gradually pour in the water and bring together to form a dough. Add the oil and knead on a clean surface for 4–5 minutes.

7. Using a rolling pin, roll and separate the dough into 6–8 golf-ball-size balls, then roll out each ball.

8. Place a heavy-based non-stick pan over a high heat and dry fry the flatbreads on each side for 1 minute until they start to colour.

9. *To serve:* top a flatbread with braised lamb, add a dollop of greek yogurt, scatter with fresh coriander and decorate with pickled radish. Ideally, serve with herby couscous salad on a bed of roasted beetroot hummus.

CHEF'S TIP: 'FOR SUPER LIGHT AND FLUFFY FLATBREADS, APPLY PRESSURE WITH A DAMP TEA TOWEL WHILE FRYING – THIS WILL CREATE AIR POCKETS'

COFFEE PAIRING
Black americano

PLAYLIST PAIRING
Song: I Got The...
Artist: Labi Siffre

THE OX SHED

Cholsey, Oxfordshire

Popular with families, dog walkers and remote workers, The Ox Shed is a thriving neighbourhood hub in the village of Cholsey. Its reputation is so good that cyclists, ramblers on the Thames Path and even paddleboarders sweeping down the river hop off to indulge in its cakes and artisan coffee.

Most visitors plump for the house roast, a Guatemalan and Honduran blend with notes of chocolate and caramel, which is roasted in Oxfordshire by Dark Horse. If you fancy something different, there's usually also a guest option available.

The spacious venue is known for its quality local food, and visitors will find the counter laden with fresh salads, pastries, bakes and doughnuts. Visit on the weekend to take advantage of the pop-up artisan bakery and stock up on local produce.

RECIPE

BUTTERNUT SQUASH DAL WITH CRUNCHY SPICED CHICKPEAS

Butternut Squash Dal with Crunchy Spiced Chickpeas

Recipe by Tegaday Quesada of The Ox Shed

Serves **6–8**
Preparation time **5–10 minutes** (plus overnight radish pickling)
Cooking time **35 minutes**

For the pickled radishes

Baby radishes 5, sliced
White wine vinegar 300ml
Caster sugar 150g
Peppercorns 1 tsp

For the dal

Butternut squash 1, peeled, deseeded and diced
Lentils 400g
Oil 1 tbsp
Onion 1, peeled and finely sliced
Red chillies 2, deseeded and finely chopped
Ginger 1 tbsp, finely diced
Garlic 1 tbsp, finely sliced
Cumin seeds 1 tbsp
Turmeric 1 tsp
Sweet paprika 1 tsp
Garam masala 1 tsp
Curry powder 1 tsp
Water 1l
Lemon 1, juice
Coconut cream 160ml
Fresh coriander a handful, chopped
Salt and pepper to taste

For the chickpeas

Chickpeas 400g tin, drained
Smoked paprika 1 tbsp

To serve

Flatbreads (see page 114 for recipe)

1. **For the pickled radishes:** in a saucepan over a medium heat, warm the vinegar and sugar and stir until the sugar dissolves. Remove from the heat, stir in the radishes and allow to cool.

2. Decant into a sterilised jar, add the peppercorns and leave to pickle overnight (this will keep for 3 months in the fridge).

3. **For the dal:** preheat the oven to 180°C / gas 4. Put the squash on an oven tray, drizzle with oil and roast for 30 minutes.

4. Put the lentils in a sieve and rinse with cold water.

5. Heat the oil in a frying pan over a medium heat. Add the onions and fry for 10–12 minutes until soft. Add the chillies, ginger, garlic and spices to the pan and cook for 2–3 minutes.

6. Add the lentils and water, bring to a simmer and cook for 30–35 minutes, skimming off any foam with a spoon. Add the roasted squash, lemon juice and coconut cream. Season to taste.

7. **For the chickpeas:** preheat the oven to 170°C / gas 3. Combine the chickpeas and smoked paprika then roast for 30 minutes. Toss halfway through cooking.

8. **To serve:** place the dal in a bowl and top with roasted chickpeas. Sprinkle fresh coriander on top and serve with sliced flatbreads and pickled radishes.

CHEF'S TIP: 'SEASON THE DAL JUST BEFORE SERVING AS ADDING SALT WHILE COOKING WILL TOUGHEN THE LENTILS'

COFFEE PAIRING
Coconut-milk latte

PLAYLIST PAIRING
Song: Another Lover
Artist: Little Dragon

VOYAGER COFFEE

Buckfastleigh, Devon

To minimise the footprint of its coffee, this Devon roastery uses 100 per cent compostable packaging (made from renewable plant starch). It also collects used packaging from its wholesale customers which it composts at the roastery.

Voyager is just as careful about waste from its roasting process and employs a zero-to-landfill approach, composting and recycling wherever possible.

As you'd expect, the Voyager team source with integrity too: the majority of their single origins and blends are obtained from small or organic farms and cooperatives via partnerships with experts in ethical sourcing. These planet-friendly practices combine with accomplished roasting skills and barista talent to create the kind of coffee that wins accolades – and lots of them.

RECIPE

COFFEE-GLAZED BARBECUE SHORT RIBS AND SLAW

COFFEE-GLAZED BARBECUE SHORT RIBS AND SLAW

Recipe by Voyager Coffee and Luca Berardino of Andria Restaurant

Serves **8**
Preparation time **45 minutes**
Cooking time **13.5 hours**

For the ribs

Salt 2 tbsp
Cracked black pepper 1 tbsp
Smoked paprika 2 tsp
Garlic powder 1 tsp
English beef short ribs 1½ kg, bones removed, cut into 8 portions

For the coffee glaze

Butter 100g
Onions 5 medium, peeled and finely sliced
Soft dark brown sugar 200g
Salt 2 large pinches
High-quality beef stock 1½ litre
Glucose syrup 1 tbsp
Hickory barbecue sauce 100g
Honey 100g
Rose harissa 30g
Espresso (we use Voyager Fat Roc espresso blend) 120–150g or 3 double espressos
Cracked black pepper 10 turns

For the slaw

Carrots 2, peeled and sliced into thin strips
Pak choi 2, sliced into thin strips
Salt 1 large pinch
Sesame oil 1 tbsp
Lime ½, juice
Roasted peanuts 3 tbsp, crushed
Roasted sesame seeds 1 tbsp

1. *For the ribs:* in a large bowl, combine the salt, pepper, paprika and garlic. Add the ribs and rub the seasoning into the meat. Individually wrap each portion in baking parchment, then tightly wrap in kitchen foil. Put the portions on an oven tray and cook in the oven at 90°C / gas 1 for 13 hours.

2. *For the coffee glaze:* put the butter, onions, 100g of sugar and a pinch of salt in a saucepan over a high heat. Cook for 5 minutes, then lower the heat and cook for a further 2 hours. Stir frequently to prevent the onions from catching. Remove from the heat once the onions have reduced to a rich, sticky jam. Set aside.

3. Put the beef stock and glucose in a saucepan over a high heat and reduce the liquid by ⅔ until thick and glossy. If the sauce is too thin and won't coat a spoon, add a further 2 tbsps of glucose.

4. Add the remaining ingredients and the sticky onions to the reduced beef stock. Simmer for 2 minutes then put in a blender and blitz until smooth. Set aside.

5. Remove the beef from the oven and increase the temperature to 200°C / gas 6.

6. Unwrap the beef then smother it in most of the coffee glaze (reserving 3–4 tbsp for basting) and return it to the oven for 15–20 minutes. Baste with the remaining sauce halfway through.

7. *For the slaw:* season the vegetables with the salt. Stir in the remaining ingredients.

8. *To serve:* place each portion of the glazed short ribs in the centre of a plate and top with 1 tbsp of slaw.

CHEF'S TIP: 'THIS SAUCE IS GREAT WITH ALMOST ANYTHING – SLATHER IT ON RIBS, WINGS OR YOUR FAVOURITE BARBECUED VEGGIES'

COFFEE PAIRING

Iced long black with fresh lime

PLAYLIST PAIRING

Song: Player Of Games
Artist: Grimes

BAKES, CAKES & DESSERTS

PIÑA COLADA CAKE	128
ANZAC BISCUITS	134
HAZELNUT CARAMEL SLICE	138
BLACKBERRY AND ROSE CAKE	142
MILE-HIGH LEMON MERINGUE PIE	146
STEM GINGER CAKE	150
TIRAMISU CAKE	154
LEMON BUNS	160
COOKIES AND CREAM CHOCOLATE CAKE	164
WHITE SOURDOUGH	170

STRONG ADOLFOS

Wadebridge, Cornwall

Since 2013, this indie cafe has been a haven for day-trippers and staycationers travelling along the Atlantic Highway in Cornwall. Unlike many other roadside stops in the country, Strong Adolfos is the kind of place you dream of stumbling upon to break up a long journey.

Founders John and Mathilda Friström Eldridge have created a welcoming and contemporary space where visitors can relax and revive. Quirky additions to the sleek decor reference their passions for surf and motorcycle culture, and add a personal touch to the experience.

Top-notch espresso drinks are complemented by an eye-widening selection of bakes, many of which are inspired by Mathilda's Scandinavian heritage. If something more substantial is needed to fuel onward adventures, Strong Adolfos' award-winning menu of breakfast, brunch and lunch dishes will fit the bill.

RECIPE
PIÑA COLADA CAKE

PIÑA COLADA CAKE

CHEF'S TIP: 'FOR EXTRA STABILITY, CUT A PAPER STRAW SLIGHTLY SHORTER THAN THE HEIGHT OF THE TRIPLE-LAYER CAKE AND DRIVE IT THROUGH THE CENTRE OF THE THREE ICED SPONGES'

COFFEE PAIRING

Flat white

PLAYLIST PAIRING

Song: Shanghai

Artist: King Gizzard & The Lizard Wizard

PIÑA COLADA CAKE

Recipe by Samantha Warwick
of Strong Adolfos

Serves **10–12**
Preparation time **40 minutes**
Cooking time **25 minutes**

You will need

20cm round cake tins 3

For the cake

Desiccated coconut 110g
Unsalted butter 260g, softened
Soft light brown sugar 260g
Vanilla bean paste 1 tsp
Free-range eggs 5
Self-raising flour 260g
Baking powder 1½ tsp
Pineapple chunks 432g tin, drained (juice reserved) and blitzed in a food processor

For the sugar syrup

Caster sugar 50g
Water 50ml
Reserved pineapple juice or dark rum 1 tbsp

For the icing

Unsalted butter 80g, softened
Icing sugar 400g
Mascarpone 150g
Vanilla bean paste ½ tsp
Reserved pineapple juice or dark rum 1 tsp
White chocolate 75g, melted and cooled

Optional decorations

Desiccated coconut
Edible flowers
Dehydrated pineapple slices
Lime zest
Fresh mint leaves

1. **For the cake:** preheat the oven to 180°C / gas 4. Grease the cake tins and line with baking parchment.

2. Spread the desiccated coconut on a baking tray. Toast in the oven for 3–5 minutes until just starting to bronze. Keep an eye on it as it can burn quickly. Remove from the oven and leave to cool.

3. Using a stand mixer or electric whisk, beat the butter, sugar and vanilla until pale and fluffy. Add the eggs, one at a time, adding a tbsp of the flour between each egg to prevent the mixture from curdling.

4. Using a spatula, carefully fold in the remaining flour, baking powder and 75g of the cooled toasted coconut. Once combined, fold in the blitzed pineapple.

5. Split the mixture evenly between the three cake tins and bake for approximately 25 minutes until the sponges are springy to the touch and skewers come out clean. Remove from the oven and put on a wire tray to cool (still in tins).

6. **For the sugar syrup:** put the sugar and water in a small saucepan over a low heat. Once all the sugar granules have dissolved, remove from the heat and add the reserved pineapple juice or dark rum.

7. Once the cakes have slightly cooled, lightly prick the surface of the sponges with a cocktail stick and liberally brush the syrup over them using a pastry brush. Leave the cakes in the tins to cool completely.

8. **For the icing:** put the butter, icing sugar, mascarpone, vanilla and pineapple juice or dark rum in a mixing bowl. Using a stand mixer or electric whisk, mix the icing until it's light and fluffy. Add the melted white chocolate and combine.

9. **To assemble:** place one of the cakes on a cake stand or a plate. Using a piping bag or palette knife, evenly spread ⅓ of the icing on top. Layer with another cake and icing, then repeat.

10. Decorate the top of the cake with the remaining toasted coconut and any optional extras such as edible flowers, dehydrated pineapple slices, lime zest or fresh mint leaves.

KOOKABURRA BAKEHOUSE

Chester, Cheshire

With extra time on her hands during lockdown, Sydney-born Jessica Reynolds taught herself how to make sourdough. What started as a pandemic project quickly turned into a fully fledged career when she began supplying local cafes and wholesalers with her fresh bakes.

Then, in 2021, the perfect premises came up and Jess took the plunge, opening a bakehouse with her fellow business owners Ian and Nicole McArdle. The unique hangout pays homage to Jess' Aussie roots: it's named after the Australian bird and has the laid-back vibe and speciality coffee you'd find in one of Sydney's urban cafes.

The crew use locally sourced ingredients to create the line-up found on the weekly changing menu. Chewy sourdough, golden pastries and moreish biscuits sit alongside cruffins oozing with next-level flavours such as Biscoff custard, strawberry cheesecake mousse, and lemon meringue.

RECIPE

ANZAC BISCUITS

ANZAC BISCUITS

Recipe by Jessica Reynolds of Kookaburra Bakehouse

Makes **10**
Preparation time **15 minutes**
Cooking time **12 minutes**

Butter 250g
Caster sugar 165g
Golden syrup 50g
Plain flour 60g
Oats 165g
Desiccated coconut 165g
Bicarbonate of soda 5g
Ground cinnamon 2 tsp
Ground ginger 1 tsp

1. Preheat the oven to 180°C / gas 4.
2. Melt the butter in a heavy-based saucepan over a low heat. Whisk in the sugar and golden syrup then set aside to cool.
3. Sieve the flour into a large bowl. Add the rest of the dry ingredients and combine.
4. Pour the butter mixture over the dry ingredients and stir to combine.
5. Roll the mixture into 10 palm-size balls. Place the balls on a lined baking tray, ensuring there's enough space between them as they will spread. Place in the oven.
6. Remove after 8 minutes and reshape the biscuits using the back of a spoon. Bake for a further 6–8 minutes depending on the desired chewiness.

CHEF'S TIP: 'TO ACHIEVE PERFECT ANZAC BISCUITS, RESHAPE THEM INTO CIRCLES WHILE THEY'RE STILL WARM'

COFFEE PAIRING

Ozone Coffee flat white

PLAYLIST PAIRING

Song: In the Summertime
Artist: Thirsty Merc

BAKES, CAKES & DESSERTS

NUMBER THIRTEEN COFFEE HOUSE & CAKERY

Knaresborough, Yorkshire

Like many cafe owners, it was time spent working as a barista in New Zealand that inspired Sarah Ward to open her own coffee shop.

She took the plunge in 2018 and it paid off: her retro-style coffee house and cakery in Knaresborough becoming a busy hub. Legions of locals and tourists swing by to slurp delicious brews made from showstopping Roost-roasted beans.

Pretty much everything inside the cafe is handmade, preloved or upcycled, and most of the furnishings sourced from auction houses, charity shops or car-boot sales. The quirky surroundings are the perfect setting for anyone looking to linger over a silky flat white with a slab of cake, and have resulted in the cafe gaining an Excellence in Business Award for its eco credentials.

RECIPE

HAZELNUT CARAMEL SLICE

HAZELNUT CARAMEL SLICE

Recipe by Sarah Ward of
Number Thirteen Coffee House & Cakery

Makes **12–14**
Preparation time **20 minutes**
Cooking time **30–45 minutes**

You will need

20 × 30cm brownie tin

For the base

Dairy-free butter 200g

Soft brown sugar 200g

Golden syrup 75g

Cocoa powder 100g

Gluten-free plain flour 150g

Ground almonds 100g

Desiccated coconut 75g

For the caramel

Dairy-free butter 180g

Icing sugar 150g

Light brown soft sugar 100g

Golden syrup 60g

Vegan condensed milk 340g can

Roasted hazelnuts 150g, roughly chopped

For the topping

Dark chocolate 350g, broken into pieces

Vegetable oil 15ml

1. Preheat the oven to 180°C / gas 4. Line the brownie tin with baking parchment.

2. *For the base:* melt the butter, sugar and syrup in a saucepan over a medium heat, stirring until melted.

3. Remove from the heat and sift in the cocoa powder, flour, almonds and coconut. Mix until combined then firmly press into the prepared tin using the back of a spoon.

4. Bake for 15–20 minutes until the base is firm to the touch.

5. *For the caramel:* melt the butter in a heavy-based saucepan over a medium heat. Add the sugars, syrup and condensed milk then turn down the heat.

6. Stir the mixture slowly until it's bubbling. Remove from the heat for a moment and allow to settle, then return to the heat. Repeat this process until the caramel is thick and golden – this will take about 15 minutes. The caramel will set as it chills, so don't worry if it doesn't appear to be thick enough.

7. Stir the hazelnuts into the caramel and combine. Pour the caramel over the cooked base, level out, then refrigerate until set.

8. *For the topping:* melt the chocolate in a heat-proof bowl over gently boiling water. Add the oil, stir until combined and pour over the chilled caramel layer. Return to the fridge for 2–3 hours to set.

9. *To serve:* slice into portions using a hot knife – this stops the chocolate from cracking.

CHEF'S TIP: 'THIS IS A GREAT GLUTEN- AND DAIRY-FREE RECIPE, BUT YOU CAN SWAP IN CONVENTIONAL FLOUR, BUTTER AND CONDENSED MILK AND IT WILL TASTE JUST AS GOOD'

COFFEE PAIRING

Roost Coffee & Roastery's Tonto Espresso Blend oat-milk flat white

PLAYLIST PAIRING

Song: Send Me On My Way
Artist: Rusted Root

IDLE HANDS SHOP & BAKERY

Dunlop, East Ayrshire

This is the kind of place you might visit with the sole intention of picking up a coffee, only to find yourself leaving with arms spilling over with just-baked sourdough, deli goodies and coffee beans for your home hopper.

This village shop and bakery is a treasure trove of speciality coffee, oven-fresh treats, and unusual foodie gems from across the world. Dunlop locals and visitors rock up as soon as the doors open and the shop sees a steady stream of customers until closing time.

No matter what time you visit, a cracking cup of coffee awaits. Traceability is top of the team's priorities and they source single-origin lots and blends from Italian roastery Mokaflor, which shares the same sustainability values.

RECIPE

BLACKBERRY AND ROSE CAKE

BLACKBERRY AND ROSE CAKE

Recipe by Morven Kerr from Idle Hands Shop & Bakery

Serves **12**
Preparation time **30 minutes**
Cooking time **45 minutes**

You will need

20cm springform cake tin

For the cake

Free-range eggs 4
Light brown soft sugar 100g
Caster sugar 100g
Natural yogurt 100g
Olive oil 100ml
Vanilla extract 1 tsp
Rose extract ½ tsp
Lemon extract ½ tsp
Orange 1, zest
Self-raising flour 125g
Ground almonds 100g
Blackberries 250g

For the icing

Double cream 200ml
Icing sugar 4 tbsp
Rose essence ½ tsp
Mascarpone 250g
Pink food colouring

To decorate

Blackberries
Edible flowers such as violas or dried rose petals

1. Preheat the oven to 160°C / gas 3. Line the base and sides of the cake tin with baking parchment.
2. Beat the eggs and sugars with a hand-held electric whisk for 5 minutes until thick and creamy.
3. Add the yogurt, olive oil, extracts and orange zest then beat again.
4. Using a spatula, gently fold in the self-raising flour and ground almonds until combined.
5. Add the blackberries and gently fold through, being careful not to break them down too much.
6. Pour the mixture into the lined tin and bake in the centre of the oven for 45–50 minutes.
7. When cooked, allow to cool before carefully removing from the tin.
8. *For the icing:* whisk the double cream and icing sugar in a stand mixer until it just begins to thicken.
9. Add the rose essence and food colouring (just enough for a hint of pink) and mix. Add the mascarpone, a large spoonful at a time. Whisk until it's smooth and has achieved a good consistency for spreading, being careful not to overbeat.
10. Spread the icing over the cooled cake, then decorate with flowers and berries.

CHEF'S TIP: 'IF YOU'VE OVERWHIPPED THE CREAM TOPPING, SIMPLY ADD MORE DOUBLE CREAM AND FOLD WITH A SPATULA UNTIL IT BECOMES SMOOTH AND LIGHT'

COFFEE PAIRING

Guggenheimer Supreme Beans double ristretto

PLAYLIST PAIRING

Song: All Blues
Artist: Miles Davis

PUREKNEAD

Whitley Bay, Tyne and Wear

Take a stroll along Whitley Bay's Park View and the waft of freshly baked pastries and just-ground coffee is likely to draw you into this popular venue.

PureKnead founder Paula Watson started selling her baked goods at Tynemouth Market in 2015. The lovingly crafted pastries, cakes and loaves were such a hit that two years later, when the opportunity arose for her to take over a former laundrette, she launched this cafe-bakery.

A daily haul of cinnamon-dusted buns, 48-hour sourdough loaves and crisp croissants has seen the bakery garner a loyal fanbase. People make a beeline for the coffee too: London's Square Mile provides a high-quality espresso blend and selection of single origins which are served as pourover and AeroPress.

Check out PureKnead's sister bakery on Dean Street in Newcastle for more homemade spoils.

RECIPE

MILE-HIGH LEMON MERINGUE PIE

MILE-HIGH LEMON MERINGUE PIE

Recipe by PureKnead

Serves **8–10**
Preparation time **1 hour 25 minutes**
Cooking time **1 hour 25 minutes**

You will need

20cm round tin (a deep quiche tin works well)

For the pastry

Plain flour 225g

Semolina or ground almonds 5 tbsp

Icing sugar 120g

Cold unsalted butter 170g, cubed

Free-range eggs 1 medium

Free-range egg yolk 1, beaten

For the lemon filling

Lemon juice 285ml

Lemons 2, zest

Granulated sugar 450g

Free-range eggs 6

Plain flour 65g

Free-range egg yolk 1, beaten

Salt a pinch

For the meringue

Free-range egg whites 180g, room temperature

Caster sugar 450g

Water 180g

1. *For the pastry:* in a large bowl, combine the flour, semolina (or ground almonds) and icing sugar. Add the butter and rub into the flour mixture until it resembles fine breadcrumbs. Add the eggs one at a time until the pastry comes together when squeezed – you don't want it to be too sticky. Wrap the bowl with clingfilm or greaseproof paper and chill it in the fridge for 30 minutes.

2. Preheat the oven to 180°C / gas 4. On a floured surface, roll out the pastry to the thickness of a pound coin. Place in the baking tin, gently pressing the pastry into the corners – if it tears, gently push it together to fill any gaps. Place in the fridge for 30 minutes.

3. Line the pastry with greaseproof paper, cover with baking beans and bake for approximately 30 minutes until the top edges turn golden. Remove the beans and paper, then gently prick the pastry base with a fork. Glaze with the egg yolk to waterproof the pastry and return to the oven for 5 minutes.

4. *For the lemon filling:* preheat the oven to 145°C / gas 1. In a saucepan over a low-medium heat, combine the lemon juice, zest and sugar and gently heat until the sugar dissolves. In a bowl, whisk together the eggs and flour, then pour the hot lemon mix into it, whisking continuously. Pour the lemon filling into the pastry case and bake for approximately 35 minutes until set. Chill it in the fridge for 1–2 hours, or overnight.

5. *For the meringue:* in a clean bowl (use a stand mixer if you have one), whisk the egg whites until they form stiff peaks. In a saucepan, combine the sugar and water and heat to 116°C. Pour the sugar mixture into the egg whites and gently whisk until incorporated. Leave to cool.

6. Spoon the meringue on top of the lemon filling, swirl with the back of a wet spoon to shape. Use a blow torch, or put in a hot oven, to brown. Serve chilled.

CHEF'S TIP: 'IF YOU CAN'T BE BOTHERED TO ZEST THE LEMONS, PARE ROUGHLY WITH A VEGETABLE PEELER, PUT IN A FOOD PROCESSOR WITH THE SUGAR, AND BLITZ'

COFFEE PAIRING
Americano

PLAYLIST PAIRING
Song: Learn to Fly
Artist: Foo Fighters

DARK WOODS COFFEE

Huddersfield, Yorkshire

The unwavering quality of Dark Woods' coffee is evidenced by numerous Great Taste awards – including two of its coveted Golden Forks (the food and drink equivalent of an Oscar) – and being a finalist in the BBC Food and Farming Awards (Best Drinks Producer 2021).

Since it was established in 2013, the roastery has blazed a trail of coffee beans across the North, pairing with cafes and restaurants to bring speciality coffee to the people. Its beans are also available online, direct from the roastery and via a network of artisan stockists, while the team's expertise can be tapped via their SCA-accredited courses.

As one of the first roasteries in the industry to be certified as a B Corp, Dark Woods has formalised its commitment to operate as a force for good. Over the years the team have nurtured long-term relationships with exceptional coffee producers across the world.

RECIPE
STEM GINGER CAKE

STEM GINGER CAKE

Recipe by Paul Meikle-Janney of
Dark Woods Coffee

Serves **8–10**
Preparation time **30–45 minutes**
Cooking time **30 minutes**

You will need

30 × 23 × 4cm loaf tin

For the cake

Salted butter 250g, softened

Black treacle 120g

Dark muscovado sugar 250g

Plain flour 375g

Ground ginger 5 tbsp

Ground cinnamon 2 tsp

Crystallised stem ginger 4 pieces, minced

Free-range eggs 2, beaten

Whole milk 300ml

Bicarbonate of soda 2 tsp

For the icing

Salted butter 100g, softened

Icing sugar 200g

Cream cheese 250g

Crystallised stem ginger 6 pieces, roughly chopped

Syrup from the crystallised ginger a drizzle

1. *For the cake:* preheat the oven to 160°C / gas 3. Line the tin with baking parchment.

2. In a small saucepan, gently heat the butter, treacle and sugar until the butter has melted and the mixture is smooth. Set aside to cool slightly.

3. In a large mixing bowl, combine the flour, ground ginger and cinnamon. Pour in the treacle mixture and give it a good stir, then stir in the stem ginger and eggs.

4. Gently warm the milk in a saucepan, add the bicarbonate of soda and allow it to foam. Slowly pour into the cake mixture and stir until incorporated.

5. Pour the mixture into the prepared tin and bake for 30 minutes, or until dark golden and springy to the touch. Leave it to cool in the tin for 10 minutes before removing and placing on a wire rack to cool completely.

6. If time allows, place the cake in an airtight container and ice it the next day.

7. *For the icing:* in a bowl, mix the butter and icing sugar to form a breadcrumb-like texture. Stir in the cream cheese, stem ginger and a drizzle of the ginger syrup (don't beat the mixture as it could split).

8. Cut the cake in half lengthways. Spread half of the icing on the base, then place the other half on top of the cake. Cover with the remaining icing.

CHEF'S TIP: 'BAKING THIS IN A LOAF TIN MAKES IT EASY TO SERVE IN NEAT, EVEN PORTIONS'

COFFEE PAIRING
Dark Woods Colombia El Placer filter

PLAYLIST PAIRING
Song: Tiraquon Acid Funk
Artist: Space Dimension Controller

BAKEHOUSE AT CAKESMITHS

Bristol

This coffee shop and bakery is the cake at the end of the tunnel for cyclists completing the Bath to Bristol cycle path. Of course, you don't have to arrive on two wheels as it's also handily close to Bristol Temple Meads train station and even has a small car park.

Located on an unassuming industrial estate, Bakehouse is a busy hub of caffeine, cake and creativity. It's the home of Cakesmiths' Cake Lab, where chief cake inventor Mike Smart and his team dream up fabulous bakes. These are roadtested at the open-plan in-house bakery before being rolled out for delivery to speciality coffee shops across the UK.

Visit to watch the award-winning bakers at work while you feast on their latest inventions. Pair your pick of the cake counter with smooth espresso-based coffee from Bristol roastery Clifton.

RECIPE
TIRAMISU CAKE

TIRAMISU CAKE

CHEF'S TIP: 'MAKE THE SPONGE LAYERS AHEAD OF TIME FOR EASE. THEY CAN ALSO BE FROZEN AFTER BEING SOAKED, JUST WRAP THEM IN CLINGFILM FIRST'

COFFEE PAIRING

Cold brew

PLAYLIST PAIRING

Song: Che La Luna
Artist: Louis Prima

TIRAMISU CAKE

Recipe by Charity Vincent
and Mike Smart of Cakesmiths

Serves **12–16**
Preparation time **2–3 hours**
Cooking time **20–25 minutes**

You will need

22cm round cake tins 3

For the cake

Salted butter 190g
Rapeseed oil 190g
Golden syrup 190g
Dark chocolate (we use 70 per cent) 300g
Free-range eggs 6, at room temperature
Warm water 70ml
Light brown soft sugar 375g
Plain flour 225g
Cocoa powder 90g
Baking powder 1 tsp

For the rum-coffee soak

Water 400g
Instant coffee powder 15g
Caster sugar 200g
Dark rum 30g

For the mascarpone filling

Mascarpone 450g
Icing sugar 100g

For the milk-chocolate coffee ganache

Milk chocolate 200g
Double cream 160g
Golden syrup 30g
Coffee beans a handful

For the dark-chocolate ganache

Dark chocolate 180g
Double cream 180g
Golden syrup 30g

For the gold coffee beans (optional)

Coffee beans a handful
Edible gold lustre a pinch

1. *For the cake:* preheat the oven to 160°C / gas 3. Grease the cake tins and line with baking parchment.

2. Melt the butter, oil, golden syrup and dark chocolate in a bowl over simmering water, mixing with a spatula until combined.

3. Crack the eggs into a clean bowl, whisk with a fork until smooth, then add the warm water and whisk until combined. Set aside.

4. Put all of the dry ingredients in a clean mixing bowl (or a stand mixer) and combine. Add the melted chocolate mix, then stir again until combined.

5. Add the egg and water mixture and beat until glossy and the beaters leave a trail on the surface of the mixture when lifted (ribbon stage).

6. Portion the mixture evenly between the three cake tins. Bake for 20–25 minutes, or until a skewer comes out clean. Once cooked, allow to cool completely and then remove from the tins. If the cakes have peaked in the centre, carefully slice off the peaks using a sharp bread knife.

7. *For the rum-coffee soak:* put the water, instant coffee and sugar in a saucepan and bring to the boil. Remove from the heat, stir in the rum and leave to cool.

8. *For the mascarpone filling:* put the mascarpone and icing sugar in a stand mixer. Mix at medium speed until combined and has no lumps. Be careful not to over mix.

9. Turn the mixer down to a low speed, then slowly add 50ml of the rum-coffee soak and mix until just combined.

10. *For the milk-chocolate coffee ganache:* put the chocolate in a heatproof bowl. In a saucepan, heat the double cream, golden syrup and coffee beans until just below boiling. Just before the cream starts to boil, strain through a sieve onto the chocolate.

11. Let this sit for 1 minute and then whisk gently until smooth. Set aside to cool.

12. *For the dark-chocolate ganache:* repeat the same process as for the milk-chocolate coffee ganache (you won't need to sieve this as it doesn't include coffee beans).

13. *For the gold coffee beans (if using):* put the coffee beans and gold lustre in a container and give it a good shake until the coffee beans are coated.

14. *To assemble:* using a pastry brush or a plastic squeeze bottle, saturate each of the sponges with the remaining chilled coffee-rum soak.

15. Place one cake on a cake stand or plate and spoon half of the mascarpone filling on top. Using a palette knife, spread the filling evenly over the top of the cake. Place the second cake on top, followed by the remaining mascarpone filling, then top with the final cake.

16. *To decorate:* fill a piping bag (with a star-shaped nozzle) with one of the ganaches and pipe randomly onto the cake. Pipe enough to fill half of the top of the cake. Vary the size by applying more pressure to the piping bag.

17. Fill a separate piping bag (using the same star-shape nozzle) with the other ganache and fill in the gaps until the top of the cake is covered. Decorate the cake with the gold coffee beans. Chill for a minimum of 2 hours before slicing and serving.

FINCA

Poundbury, Dorset

At this Poundbury powerhouse, a crew of bakers craft high-calibre carbs for Finca's four artisan coffee shops across Dorset and Somerset.

The irresistible smell of hot-from-the-oven bread draws crowds from the crack of dawn, and is accompanied by the arresting aroma of just-ground speciality coffee. The beans are also the handiwork of the Finca team: the seasonal line-up of single origins is bronzed at their Dorchester HQ.

In summer, visitors spill out of the hexagonal bakehouse to nab alfresco deckchairs and bierkeller benches. The terrace is a great spot for lounging while enjoying the bustle of picturesque Poundbury and simultaneously savouring a lemon bun and an expertly prepared coffee.

RECIPE

LEMON BUNS

LEMON BUNS

Recipe by Don Iszatt of Finca

Serves **12**
Cooking time **15 minutes**
Preparation time **1 hour 45 minutes**
(plus overnight proving time)

You will need

Stand mixer (with a dough attachment)

30 × 40cm baking tray

For the buns

Plain flour 1kg

Caster sugar 75g

Salt 18g

Dried yeast 7g

Lukewarm water 530ml

Lemon essence 15ml

Butter 160g, softened

Lemon curd 300g, chilled

For the lemon topping

Lemon juice 60ml

Caster sugar 120g

Poppy seeds 1 tsp

1. *For the buns:* put the flour, sugar, salt and yeast in a stand mixer and mix for 20 seconds.

2. In a separate bowl, combine the water and lemon essence. Add it to the dry ingredients and mix at a slow speed for 5 minutes, or until all of the ingredients are combined and the mixture pulls away from the sides of the bowl.

3. Add ⅓ of the butter and mix again until combined. Repeat this process twice to incorporate the rest of the butter.

4. Take the dough out of the mixer and place in a clean bowl. Cover with clingfilm and leave to prove in the fridge overnight.

5. The next morning, remove the dough from the fridge and place on a lightly floured surface. Using a rolling pin, roll the dough into a rectangle approximately 30cm × 50cm, keeping the long side closest to you.

6. Spread the lemon curd evenly across the top of the dough and then roll (swiss-roll style) lengthways away from you.

7. Using a knife, cut the roll evenly into 12 pieces. The easiest way is to cut the roll in half, then in half again, then cut each quarter into three.

8. Line the baking tray with baking parchment and place the buns on the tray, leaving an even gap between the buns and the tray edges. Put in the fridge, uncovered, to chill for 30 minutes.

9. Preheat the oven to 60°C. Put the buns in the oven, leaving the door open, for approximately 30 minutes for the dough to prove. The buns should expand to fill the gaps and become warm and soft to the touch.

10. Once proved, bake the buns in the oven at 180°C / gas 4 for 14–16 minutes or until they are golden brown.

11. *For the lemon topping:* place the lemon juice and caster sugar in a bowl and mix with a spoon until the sugar has dissolved.

12. While the buns are still warm, use a brush to generously glaze them with the lemon topping, then sprinkle with poppy seeds. Once cooled, use a knife to separate the buns.

CHEF'S TIP: 'THESE BUNS DELIVER A TRIPLE LEMON HIT: ZESTY DOUGH, CURD FILLING AND DRIZZLE TOPPING'

COFFEE PAIRING

Espresso

PLAYLIST PAIRING

Song: Don't Let Me Be Misunderstood
Artist: Valerie Broussard

PELICANO COFFEE CO.

Brighton, Sussex

A coffee-shop tour of Brighton isn't complete without a trip to at least one of the Pelicano cafes.

Its flagship outlet on Sydney Street is, appropriately enough, where founders Zephir Thomas and Sol Lee set up their first speciality coffee shop after being inspired by the Australian scene. Fast-forward eight years and the small hangout has been joined by two sister locations at The Level and on Lewes Road. As a result of buying in so much coffee, the gang decided to take the roasting operation in-house and now also supply flavour-popping beans to other businesses.

A lip-smacking selection of coffees for filter and espresso are cooked up on a 24kg Kuban and are available to sample at Pelicano cafes and beyond.

RECIPE
COOKIES AND CREAM CHOCOLATE CAKE

CHEF'S TIP: 'ENSURE THE ICING HAS BEEN THOROUGHLY BEATEN SO IT'S ULTRA SMOOTH AND FLUFFY'

COFFEE PAIRING

Pelicano Smokey Bird Espresso Blend flat white

PLAYLIST PAIRING

Song: Sink into the Floor

Artist: Feng Suave

COOKIES AND CREAM CHOCOLATE CAKE

Recipe by Gwen Stanbrook of Pelicano Coffee Co.

Serves **12**
Preparation time **25 minutes**
Cooking time **30–35 minutes**

You will need

22cm round cake tins 2

For the chocolate cake

Plain flour 580g

Granulated sugar 800g

Cocoa powder 200g

Bicarbonate of soda 3 tsp

Baking powder 1 tsp

Free-range eggs 5, lightly beaten

Vegetable oil 300ml

Warm water 400ml

Milk 490ml

For the cookies and cream icing

Unsalted butter 250g, softened

Icing sugar 600g

Oreos 2 packets, 1 packet with the biscuits chopped into tiny pieces, the other cut into halves

White chocolate 25g

1. *For the chocolate cake:* preheat the oven to 180°C / gas 4. Grease the cake tins and line with baking parchment.

2. In a large mixing bowl, combine the flour, sugar, cocoa powder, bicarbonate of soda and baking powder.

3. Add the eggs and oil then mix to combine. Continue to mix while slowly adding the warm water, then slowly add the milk.

4. Once the mixture is smooth, split it between the cake tins and bake in the oven for 30–35 minutes until they are firm to the touch and a skewer comes out clean.

5. Remove the cakes from the oven and leave to cool slightly in the tins, then transfer onto wire racks to cool completely.

6. *For the cookies and cream icing:* put the butter and icing sugar in a bowl, then beat until light and fluffy. Stir in the small Oreo pieces.

7. *To assemble:* if the cakes have peaked, carefully slice the peaks off with a sharp knife to make a level surface.

8. Place one cake on a cake stand or plate and spread a couple of spoonfuls of the icing on top. Place the other sponge on top of the icing and cover with the rest of the icing, spreading it evenly across the top and sides of the cake. Decorate with the Oreo halves.

9. Place the white chocolate in a heatproof bowl. Microwave on a high heat in 15 second bursts, stirring between each blast, until melted.

10. Drizzle the white chocolate over the cake, let the chocolate set and then serve.

ELECTRIC BAKERY

Bude, Cornwall

Locals (and not-so-locals) have flocked to this out-of-town bakery since it opened in 2019, its fanbase spreading faster than cookie dough on a hot baking tray.

This is a mostly takeaway set-up although its outside seating is an opportunity to sit in the sun and scoff lunchtime specials such as miso-roasted chicken leg and squash served with white bean and celeriac cassoulet, braised winter greens, roast garlic and chilli mayo – plus a wedge of springy focaccia.

House espresso beans are fresh from Cornwall's Origin roastery, and supported by a handful of rotating guest batch and cold brews.

On the bakery front, double-doughnut specials are the ultimate indulgence, closely followed by Electric's cinnamon buns. And as for the speciality sourdough, soda and yeasted breads? Well, let's just say it's worth getting there early.

RECIPE
WHITE SOURDOUGH

WHITE SOURDOUGH

Recipe by Benedict Harding and Alex Bluett of Electric Bakery

Serves **4**
Preparation time **30 minutes (plus proving time)**
Cooking time **50–70 minutes**

You will need

Dough scraper

Banneton / proving basket

Double-edge razor (a tomato knife works well too)

For the sourdough

Strong white bread flour (we use Shipton Mill's No.4) 500g

Spelt or light rye flour 50g

Sourdough starter 200g

Salt 15g

Water 300ml

Vegetable oil

Semolina a few handfuls

1. In a large bowl, roughly mix together the flours, starter, salt and water. Turn out onto a lightly floured surface and knead for 10 minutes until the dough is smooth and silky.

2. Lightly oil a clean bowl with vegetable oil. Put the dough in the bowl, covering it with a damp tea towel. Leave it to prove at room temperature for 3 hours.

3. During the proving time, fold the dough in half over itself, rotate it 45 degrees and repeat twice. Do this 3 times (with a 45-minute rest in between). After proving for about 3 hours the dough should have expanded a considerable amount and feel springy when poked (the amount of time this takes depends on the room temperature). Once it gets to this stage, cover the bowl with clingfilm and put it in the fridge to rest for 2–3 hours.

4. Place the rested dough on a lightly floured surface and reshape it. Lightly flatten it, pulling all of the sides into the middle, flipping it and rolling it around the work surface to form a tight, smooth ball. It might be helpful to watch a video online on shaping bread for guidance.

5. Heavily flour the proving basket. Flip the dough so it's seam-side up in the basket (smoothest side at the bottom of the basket) and place back in the fridge (uncovered) to prove overnight.

6. The next morning, preheat the oven to 240°C / gas 9. Place a deep roasting pan at the bottom of the oven.

7. Liberally dust a baking sheet with semolina, then turn the dough out onto the baking sheet (seam facing down). Slash the top with a sharp razor or knife in a confident, swift movement – an X in the centre is a classic style. This will encourage the bread to rise in the right direction.

8. Quickly place the baking sheet into the oven and pour a pint of water into the roasting pan in the bottom of the oven. This creates steam and helps achieve a consistent rise. Bake for at least 40 minutes, then check to see if the loaf is cooked by picking it up (with oven gloves) and giving it a knock. If it sounds hollow it's done, if it sounds dull or wet pop it back in the oven for another 5 minutes then check again.

9. Once baked, place the loaf on a cooling rack and allow to cool completely. Slice and serve.

CHEF'S TIP: 'TO SLICE A SOURDOUGH EASILY INTO SLICES THAT'LL FIT IN A TOASTER: CUT THE LOAF IN HALF, LAY IT CUT-SIDE DOWN AND THEN SLICE AGAIN'

COFFEE PAIRING
Origin Coffee San Fermin french press

PLAYLIST PAIRING
Song: Let's Dance Raw
Artist: Shintaro Sakamoto

DRINKS

BLUEBERRY BAOBAB SMOOTHIE	176
COTSWOLD FOG	180
EQUATORIAL	184
ESPRESSO FLOAT	188
SAMI THE SNARE'S GINGER BREW	192
THE PILOT BURNER	196
WHERE'S DEADPOOL?	200

HUNTER GATHERER

Portsmouth, Hampshire

This foodie cafe is famed for its flat whites and cinnamon rolls, but it also cranks out lip-smacking smoothies and banging plant-based all-day brekkies. Chewy bagels stuffed with veggie fillings and banana pancakes are the house faves and in demand from first thing till close of play.

'Good coffee ain't cheap and cheap coffee ain't good' is the mantra here and every effort goes into sniffing out the best beans available. Craft House Coffee in Sussex is the ever-reliable house roaster and its bespoke blend, Industrial, is Hunter Gatherer's choice for espresso. A mix of 60 per cent natural Brazilian and 40 per cent washed Colombian beans, it has a rich body with chocolate and hazelnut notes, followed by a sweet, fruity finish and toffee aftertaste.

RECIPE
BLUEBERRY BAOBAB SMOOTHIE

BLUEBERRY BAOBAB SMOOTHIE

Recipe by Mel Byrne of Hunter Gatherer

Makes **1**
Preparation time **4 minutes**

Frozen banana ½, peeled
Blueberries 100g
Baobab powder 1 tsp
Oat milk 300ml
Maple syrup 2 tbsp

1. Place all of the ingredients in a blender and blitz for 30 seconds until smooth.
2. Pour into a tall glass and serve.

CHEF'S TIP: 'ADD A TABLESPOON OF OATS FOR A THICKER, CREAMIER CONSISTENCY AND EXTRA PROTEIN'

FOOD PAIRING
Gluten-free granola with almonds, walnuts, apricots, dates and seeds

PLAYLIST PAIRING
Song: Club Tropicana
Artist: Wham!

DRINKS

FIRE & FLOW COFFEE ROASTERS

Cirencester, Gloucestershire

Ordering a flat white can be a game of Russian roulette for plant-based coffee lovers: some beans taste phenomenal with oat milk and others just don't. The pioneering team at this Cotswolds roastery were keen to eliminate the game of chance for vegan coffee fans by releasing an espresso blend developed specifically to pair with oat milk. They even include oat-milk tasting notes on all their coffee bags.

Coffee fans can visit Fire & Flow HQ near Cirencester for tours, tastings and training. Head roaster and co-founder Callum Parsons has competed in the UK Barista Championship finals on two occasions and loves to share his knowledge and skills with budding home baristas.

RECIPE

COTSWOLD FOG

COTSWOLD FOG

Recipe by Callum Parsons of Fire & Flow Coffee Roasters

Serves **4**
Preparation time **10 minutes**

Cold water 250ml

Loose-leaf earl grey tea 12g

Coconut sugar or light brown soft sugar 20g

Oat milk 800ml

1. Put the water and tea in a heavy-based saucepan over a medium heat and gently bring to the boil. This should take around 3 minutes.
2. Add the sugar and gently stir until dissolved. Turn down the temperature so the mixture is simmering, then leave to infuse for 5 minutes.
3. Strain the tea concentrate into a jug and set aside. Discard the tea leaves.
4. Using a milk steamer, gently heat and foam the oat milk.
5. Place 50ml of the earl grey concentrate in each of 4 mugs and top with the textured oat milk.

FOOD PAIRING
Salted caramel raw bar

PLAYLIST PAIRING
Song: Plus Minus
Artist: Brandon Boyd

CHEF'S TIP: 'DON'T OWN A MILK STEAMER? HEAT THE MILK TO 65°C THEN PLACE IT IN A CLEAN CAFETIERE. PUSH THE PLUNGER UP AND DOWN QUICKLY FOR 10 SECONDS TO GENERATE FOAM'

51 DEGREES NORTH COFFEE COMPANY

Braunton, Devon

Discerning caffeine fans in need of a coffee to-go are always delighted to spy Justin Duerden's black van in and around Braunton. Those requiring a more leisurely sit-and-sip experience head to his community-minded coffee shop at a nearby gym.

Whether looking for a drink-and-dash hit or a longer dalliance, regulars know they'll find award-winning coffee crafted from expertly extracted beans (roasted by Origin in Cornwall).

Justin is on a mission to support sustainable coffee plantations and direct trade. He's also keen to give back to the people of Braunton. *'We work with local independent producers and suppliers who are passionate about their products,'* he says. *'Our ethos is to be there for the local community through good and tough times, and we've built a loyal following of customers who share our beliefs and love of good coffee.'*

RECIPE
EQUATORIAL

EQUATORIAL

Recipe by Justin Duerden of 51 Degrees North Coffee Company

Serves **1**
Preparation time **5 minutes**

Condensed milk 30ml

Whole milk 100ml

Quality black peppercorns (we use Steenbergs' Tellicherry Black Peppercorns) a pinch, ground

Palm sugar 3g

Sea salt a tiny pinch

51 Degrees North medium-roast coffee 18g, ground

To garnish

Cinnamon stick

Black pepper

Nutmeg (we use Steenbergs' Organic Nutmeg) grated

1. Put the milks, pepper, sugar and salt in a small milk jug.
2. Prepare the espresso using a 32–34 second extraction to yield a 35ml double shot.
3. Steam the milk mixture until it resembles the same texture as a flat white. Don't allow the temperature to exceed 65°C.
4. Pour the milk mixture over the espresso, then garnish with the cinnamon stick, a twist of pepper and grated nutmeg.

CHEF'S TIP: 'TWEAK THE AMOUNT OF PEPPER TO SUIT YOUR TASTE, BUT THEN ADJUST THE NUTMEG TO BALANCE IT OUT'

FOOD PAIRING
Foxcombe Bakehouse All Butter Shortbread

PLAYLIST PAIRING
Song: Adore
Artist: I:Cube

DRINKS

CAIRNGORM COFFEE

Edinburgh, Scotland

The Cairngorm Coffee story started in 2014 when founder Robi Lambie opened his first speciality coffee shop on Frederick Street in Edinburgh. Such was the demand for Cairngorm's on-point brews that, two years later, the original shop was joined by a new sister venue on Melville Street.

Once the second site was established, Robi took a sidestep into the world of roasting where he built on his passion for the art and science of speciality coffee. Before long, he'd set up a roastery and begun stocking both of his shops with own-roasted beans.

Robi, with co-owner Harris Grant and team, continues to source, then roast, high-quality beans at the Cairngorm roastery HQ in Leith. The team share the coffee with the Scottish coffee community via their cafes, webshop and wholesale arm.

RECIPE
ESPRESSO FLOAT

ESPRESSO FLOAT

Recipe by Matt Mitchell of Cairngorm Coffee

Makes **1**
Preparation time **7 minutes**

Loose-leaf earl grey tea 5g

White sugar 50g

Espresso beans 36g, ground

Ice

Freshly squeezed orange juice ½ tsp

Good quality vanilla ice cream a scoop

Fresh orange a slice

1. Pour 100ml of boiling water over the earl grey tea and leave to steep for 5 minutes.
2. Strain 50ml of the tea over the white sugar and stir to make a syrup.
3. Pull a double espresso shot.
4. Half-fill a cocktail shaker with ice. Add the espresso, 18ml of the earl grey syrup and orange juice. Shake hard to aerate the mixture.
5. Pour the mixture into a glass. Top with a scoop of vanilla ice cream and garnish with a slice of fresh orange.

CHEF'S TIP: 'WE USE A SWEET AND VIBRANT WASHED KENYAN COFFEE TO MATCH THE FLORAL CHARACTERISTICS OF THE TEA'

FOOD PAIRING

Grilled cheese sandwich with sweet chilli jam

PLAYLIST PAIRING

Song: Let Me Inside Your Head
Artist: Swim School

DRINKS

HUNDRED HOUSE COFFEE

Ludlow, Shropshire

The team at this Shropshire roastery specialise in sourcing and roasting rare single-origin coffees and unique blends.

Beans arrive at the rural roastery from a wide range of countries including Kenya, Burundi, Rwanda, Tanzania, Nicaragua and Peru, while roasting takes place on a Diedrich IR-12 roaster.

The crew's ambitions extend beyond the mighty bean, however. Alongside supporting independent creatives and inner city schools through their Art & Industry programme, founder Matthew Wade also pursues his passion for non-alcoholic cocktails (something he picked up while roasting coffee in the Middle East) by developing alt recipes at the roastery.

RECIPE

SAMI THE SNARE'S GINGER BREW

SAMI THE SNARE'S GINGER BREW

Recipe by Matthew Wade of Hundred House Coffee

Makes **1**
Preparation time **5 minutes**

Seedlip Grove 42 70ml

Ginger concentrate (we use GIMBER) 50ml

Spiced gingerbread syrup (we use Monin Pain d'Epices) 50ml

Lemon 1, juice (approx. 50ml)

Ice cubes 6

Non-alcoholic beer (we use Doom Bar Zero) 140ml

1. Put the Seedlip, ginger concentrate, gingerbread syrup, lemon juice and 2 ice cubes in an electric blender and pulse for 10–20 seconds – just long enough to crush the ice.

2. Put 4 ice cubes in a chilled beer glass.

3. Pour in the blended liquid, top with the beer and serve.

CHEF'S TIP: 'BEFORE YOU CUT AND SQUEEZE THE LEMON, ROLL IT ON THE COUNTER, PUSHING IT DOWN WITH THE PALM OF YOUR HAND, TO EXTRACT MORE JUICE'

FOOD PAIRING
Burger and fries

PLAYLIST PAIRING
Song: Sunset Sound
Artist: Pachyman

DRINKS

ROASTWORKS COFFEE CO.

Willand, Devon

When selecting beans, Roastworks founder Will Little and team hunt for character and complexity. They carefully bronze them on refurbished vintage machines – including a German G W Barth drum roaster that's been in the family for 30 years – hell-bent on finding the sweet spot where flavours purr.

The crew have discovered a number of fruity and funky lots and reserve the freakiest for The Contemporary collection. One of its most notable additions was the Colombia Café Granja La Esperanza Mokka, described by Will as *'like drinking liquid black forest gateau'*.

Roastworks is committed to making speciality coffee more accessible, which the team accomplish through engaging communication and innovative products such as Nespresso-compatible capsules.

RECIPE
THE PILOT BURNER

THE PILOT BURNER

Recipe by Roastworks Coffee Co. and The Lost Kitchen

Makes **1**
Preparation time **7 minutes**

For the coffee syrup

Filter coffee 40g, ground
Demerara sugar 100g
Water 100ml

For the cocktail

Coffee syrup 25ml
High quality bourbon 50ml
Bitters 4 dashes
Ice cube 1 large

Optional garnish

Orange peel a twist
Fresh rosemary a sprig
Soda water a splash, to taste

1. **For the coffee syrup:** put all of the ingredients in a saucepan over a medium heat and slowly bring to a simmer.

2. Once the mixture is gently simmering, remove from the heat and leave to infuse for 5 minutes. Strain through a fine sieve and leave to cool (any excess coffee syrup will last for up to 1 month in an airtight container in the fridge).

3. **For the cocktail:** pour the coffee syrup, bourbon and bitters into a glass. Add the ice and stir well using a cocktail stirrer.

4. Garnish with a twist of orange peel and a sprig of fresh rosemary. Add a splash of soda water if you want to make it a longer drink.

FOOD PAIRING

A platter of local charcuterie, smoked salmon and cream cheese blinis or a South West cheese board

PLAYLIST PAIRING

Song: Barracuda '68
Artist: Seasick Steve

CHEF'S TIP: 'SINGE THE ROSEMARY TIPS AND LEAVE TO SMOULDER FOR A SMOKY EFFECT'

DRINKS

KRA:FT KOFFEE

Wakefield, Yorkshire

KRA:FT's first customers only discovered the pop-up espresso bar when they visited the tattoo artist and barber with which it shared building space. Before long, word spread that the flat whites were as good as the fades, and the KRA:FT team moved to a permanent residence on Wood Street.

The space has an industrial-glam vibe that's all copper, wood and leather, which perfectly fits KRA:FT's dual personality as both a coffee shop and cocktail bar.

By day, the gang serve a feast of bakes, craft beers and speciality coffee. By night, the lights are dimmed and the coffee cups swapped for coupe glasses. Coffee is still king, of course, and visitors can savour speciality beans in the form of Espresso Martinis.

RECIPE
WHERE'S DEADPOOL?

WHERE'S DEADPOOL?

Recipe by Muthadi Alleyne of KRA:FT Kocktails

Makes **1**
Preparation time **5 minutes**

Citrus vodka 35ml
Lemon juice 25ml
Maraschino liqueur 20ml
Crème de violette 12½ml
Ice cubes
Large ice cube (we use a round mould) 1
Gypsophila a sprig, to decorate
Lemon twist 1

1. Place the vodka, lemon juice, maraschino liqueur and crème de violette in a cocktail shaker.
2. Top with ice cubes and shake for 10–15 seconds.
3. Double strain into a coupette glass. Add the large ice cube.
4. Garnish with the gypsophila and a twist of lemon.

CHEF'S TIP: 'PLAY WITH THE AMOUNT OF MARASCHINO LIQUEUR TO SUIT YOUR PALATE'

FOOD PAIRING

Violet-infused crème brûlée

PLAYLIST PAIRING

Song: Just the Two of Us
Artist: Bill Withers

DRINKS

THE PLAYLIST

Each cafe and roastery has hand-selected the perfect tune to pair with their dish. Here's the playlist in its entirety

Stream the full playlist on Spotify. Search for

INDY CAFE COOKBOOK VOL 2

Artist	Song
Alexi Murdoch	Orange Sky
Little Dragon	Another Lover
Bill Withers	Just the Two of Us
Brandon Boyd	Plus Minus
Coco	Last of the Loving
Cymande	Brothers on the Slide
Death Cab for Cutie	Crooked Teeth
Duran Duran	Change the Skyline
ESG	Dance
Feng Suave	Sink into the Floor
Finley Quaye	Even After All
Foo Fighters	Learn to Fly
Gil Scott-Heron	I Think I'll Call It Morning
Grimes	Player Of Games
I:Cube	Adore
King Gizzard & The Lizard Wizard	Shanghai
KIRBY	We Don't Funk
Labi Siffre	I Got The...
Lilacs	Waxahatchee
Louis Prima	Che La Luna
MF Doom	Fillet-O-Rapper
Michael Kiwanuka	You Ain't the Problem
Miles Davis	All Blues
Mioko Yamaguchi	Lover
Otis Redding	(Sittin' on) the Dock of the Bay
Pachyman	Sunset Sound
Papa Bear & His Cubs	You're So Fine
Rusted Root	Send Me On My Way
Seasick Steve	Barracuda '68
Seu Jorge	Véia
Shintaro Sakamoto	Let's Dance Raw
Simply Red	Fairground
Cleo Sol	Sunshine
Space Dimension Controller	Tiraquon Acid Funk
Steve Miller Band	Abracadabra
Swim School	Let Me Inside Your Head
Thirsty Merc	In the Summertime
Two Day Coma	Figure of 8
Valerie Broussard	Don't Let Me Be Misunderstood
Wham!	Club Tropicana

INDEX

A

Almonds
- Blackberry and rose cake — 142
- Hazelnut caramel slice — 138
- Mile-high lemon meringue pie — 146
- Nutty granola with mango compote — 52
- Roasted broccoli with tahini and cranberries — 102
- Turkish eggs — 48

Apple cider vinegar
- Eggy crumpets with chilli jam and halloumi — 76

Apples
- Courgette and pepper fritters with beetroot and apple slaw — 94

Artichoke hearts
- Glasrach pizza — 98

Avocados
- Sacred scrambled tofu — 68
- Sweet potato fritters with smashed avocado, halloumi and poached eggs — 38
- Turkish eggs — 48

B

Bananas
- Blueberry baobab smoothie — 176
- Nutty granola with mango compote — 52

Baobab
- Blueberry baobab smoothie — 176

Basil
- Smoked haddock potato cakes with kale pesto and poached eggs — 80
- Whipped ricotta on sourdough with olive, basil and sun-dried tomato tapenade — 106

Beetroot
- Courgette and pepper fritters with beetroot and apple slaw — 94

Blackberries
- Blackberry and rose cake — 142
- Nutty granola with mango compote — 52

Black treacle
- Stem ginger cake — 150

Blueberries
- Blueberry baobab smoothie — 176

Broccoli
- Roasted broccoli with tahini and cranberries — 102

Butter
- Anzac biscuits — 134
- Coffee-glazed barbecue short ribs and slaw — 122
- Lemon buns — 160
- Rhubarb crumble waffles — 34
- Smoked haddock baked eggs in a lemon, nutmeg and mustard sauce — 41
- Smoked haddock potato cakes with kale pesto and poached eggs — 80

- Thai yellow eggs with mango chutney and salted cucumber — 84
- Tiramisu french toast — 72

Butternut squash
- Butternut squash dal with crunchy spiced chickpeas — 118

C

Carrots
- Coffee-glazed barbecue short ribs and slaw — 122

Cheddar
- Veggie frittata — 60

Chickpeas
- Butternut squash dal with crunchy spiced chickpeas — 118
- Sweet potato hash — 56

Chilli jam
- Courgette and pepper fritters with beetroot and apple slaw — 94
- Sweet potato fritters with smashed avocado, halloumi and poached eggs — 38

Chorizo
- Granary sunshine toast — 44

Cocoa powder
- Cookies and cream chocolate cake — 166
- Hazelnut caramel slice — 138
- Tiramisu cake — 156
- Tiramisu french toast — 72

Coconut cream
- Butternut squash dal with crunchy spiced chickpeas — 118

Coconut milk
- Thai yellow eggs with mango chutney and salted cucumber — 84

Condensed milk
- Equatorial — 184

Courgettes
- Courgette and pepper fritters with beetroot and apple slaw — 94

Cranberries
- Roasted broccoli with tahini and cranberries — 102

Cream cheese
- Stem ginger cake — 150

Crumpets
- Eggy crumpets with chilli jam and halloumi — 76

Cucumbers
- Thai yellow eggs with mango chutney and salted cucumber — 84

D

Dark chocolate
- Hazelnut caramel slice — 138
- Tiramisu cake — 156

Desiccated coconut
- Anzac biscuits — 134
- Hazelnut caramel slice — 138
- Piña colada cake — 130

Double cream
- Blackberry and rose cake — 142
- Creamy mushrooms on toast — 64
- Rhubarb crumble waffles — 34
- Sweet potato fritters with smashed avocado, halloumi and poached eggs — 38
- Tiramisu cake — 156
- Tiramisu french toast — 72

E

Eggs
- Blackberry and rose cake — 142
- Cookies and cream chocolate cake — 166
- Courgette and pepper fritters with beetroot and apple slaw — 94
- Kimchini — 110
- Mile-high lemon meringue pie — 146
- Piña colada cake — 130
- Rhubarb crumble waffles — 34
- Smoked haddock baked eggs in a lemon, nutmeg and mustard sauce — 41
- Smoked haddock potato cakes with kale pesto and poached eggs — 80
- Stem ginger cake — 150
- Sweet potato fritters with smashed avocado, halloumi and poached eggs — 38
- Sweet potato hash — 56
- Thai yellow eggs with mango chutney and salted cucumber — 84
- Tiramisu cake — 156
- Tiramisu french toast — 72
- Turkish eggs — 48
- Veggie frittata — 60

Emmental
- Smoked haddock baked eggs in a lemon, nutmeg and mustard sauce — 41

Espresso
- Coffee-glazed barbecue short ribs and slaw — 122
- Espresso float — 188
- Tiramisu french toast — 72

F

Feta
- Veggie frittata — 60

Flour
- Anzac biscuits — 134
- Blackberry and rose cake — 142
- Cookies and cream chocolate cake — 166
- Courgette and pepper fritters with beetroot and apple slaw — 94
- Crumpets with slow-cooked portobello mushrooms, beetroot relish and rocket pesto — 88
- Glasrach pizza — 98
- Hazelnut caramel slice — 138
- Kimchini — 110
- Lamb shawarma with coriander flatbreads — 114
- Lemon buns — 160
- Mile-high lemon meringue pie — 146
- Piña colada cake — 130
- Rhubarb crumble waffles — 34
- Smoked haddock baked eggs in a lemon, nutmeg and mustard sauce — 41
- Stem ginger cake — 150
- Sweet potato fritters with smashed avocado, halloumi and poached eggs — 38
- Tiramisu cake — 156
- White sourdough — 170

G

Garlic
- Butternut squash dal with crunchy spiced chickpeas — 118
- Coffee-glazed barbecue short ribs and slaw — 122
- Crumpets with slow-cooked portobello mushrooms, beetroot relish and rocket pesto — 88
- Glasrach pizza — 98
- Lamb shawarma with coriander flatbreads — 114
- Roasted broccoli with tahini and cranberries — 102
- Sacred scrambled tofu — 68
- Smoked haddock potato cakes with kale pesto and poached eggs — 80
- Sweet potato fritters with smashed avocado, halloumi and poached eggs — 38
- Turkish eggs — 48
- Whipped ricotta on sourdough with olive, basil and sun-dried tomato tapenade — 106

Ginger
- Butternut squash dal with crunchy spiced chickpeas — 118
- Sami The Snare's ginger brew — 192
- Stem ginger cake — 150

Goat's cheese
- Courgette and pepper fritters with beetroot and apple slaw — 94

Golden syrup
- Anzac biscuits — 134
- Hazelnut caramel slice — 138
- Rhubarb crumble waffles — 34
- Tiramisu cake — 156

Gooseberries
- Rhubarb crumble waffles — 34

H

Haddock
- Smoked haddock baked eggs in a lemon, nutmeg and mustard sauce — 41
- Smoked haddock potato cakes with kale pesto and poached eggs — 80

Halloumi
- Eggy crumpets with chilli jam and halloumi — 76
- Sweet potato fritters with smashed avocado, halloumi and poached eggs — 38

Hazelnuts
- Nutty granola with mango compote — 52
- Turkish eggs — 48

K

Kale
Roasted broccoli with tahini and cranberries — 102
Smoked haddock potato cakes with kale pesto and poached eggs — 80

Kimchi
Kimchini — 110

L

Lamb
Lamb shawarma with coriander flatbreads — 114

Leeks
Glasrach pizza — 98
Smoked haddock potato cakes with kale pesto and poached eggs — 80
Veggie frittata — 60

Lemons
Blackberry and rose cake — 142
Butternut squash dal with crunchy spiced chickpeas — 118
Crumpets with slow-cooked portobello mushrooms, beetroot relish and rocket pesto — 88
Lemon buns — 160
Mile-high lemon meringue pie — 146
Nutty granola with mango compote — 52
Roasted broccoli with tahini and cranberries — 102
Sami The Snare's ginger brew — 192
Smoked haddock baked eggs in a lemon, nutmeg and mustard sauce — 41
Smoked haddock potato cakes with kale pesto and poached eggs — 80
Sweet potato hash — 56
Where's Deadpool? — 200
Whipped ricotta on sourdough with olive, basil and sun-dried tomato tapenade — 106

Lentils
Butternut squash dal with crunchy spiced chickpeas — 118
Thai yellow eggs with mango chutney and salted cucumber — 84

M

Mangoes
Thai yellow eggs with mango chutney and salted cucumber — 84

Maple syrup
Blueberry baobab smoothie — 176
Nutty granola with mango compote — 52
Tiramisu french toast — 72

Mascarpone
Blackberry and rose cake — 142
Piña colada cake — 130
Tiramisu cake — 156
Tiramisu french toast — 72

Milk
Blueberry baobab smoothie — 176
Cookies and cream chocolate cake — 166
Cotswold fog — 180
Crumpets with slow-cooked portobello mushrooms, beetroot relish and rocket pesto — 88
Eggy crumpets with chilli jam and halloumi — 76
Equatorial — 184
Hazelnut caramel slice — 138
Rhubarb crumble waffles — 34
Smoked haddock baked eggs in a lemon, nutmeg and mustard sauce — 41
Smoked haddock potato cakes with kale pesto and poached eggs — 80
Stem ginger cake — 150
Thai yellow eggs with mango chutney and salted cucumber — 84
Tiramisu cake — 156
Tiramisu french toast — 72
Turkish eggs — 48

Mozzarella
Glasrach pizza — 98

Mushrooms
Creamy mushrooms on toast — 64
Glasrach pizza — 98

O

Oats
Anzac biscuits — 134
Nutty granola with mango compote — 52
Rhubarb crumble waffles — 34

Olives
Glasrach pizza — 98
Whipped ricotta on sourdough with olive, basil and sun-dried tomato tapenade — 106

Onions
Butternut squash dal with crunchy spiced chickpeas — 118
Coffee-glazed barbecue short ribs and slaw — 122
Lamb shawarma with coriander flatbreads — 114
Sweet potato hash — 56
Thai yellow eggs with mango chutney and salted cucumber — 84

Oranges
Blackberry and rose cake — 142
Espresso float — 188
Rhubarb crumble waffles — 34
The pilot burner — 196
Tiramisu french toast — 72

Oreos
Cookies and cream chocolate cake — 166

P

Pak choi
Coffee-glazed barbecue short ribs and slaw — 122

Peppers
Courgette and pepper fritters with beetroot and apple slaw — 94
Eggy crumpets with chilli jam and halloumi — 76
Glasrach pizza — 98
Sweet potato fritters with smashed avocado, halloumi and poached eggs — 38
Veggie frittata — 60

Pineapple
Piña colada cake — 130

Pine nuts

Crumpets with slow-cooked portobello mushrooms,
beetroot relish and rocket pesto … 88

Smoked haddock potato cakes
with kale pesto and poached eggs … 80

Pistachios

Tiramisu french toast … 72

Turkish eggs … 48

Potatoes

Thai yellow eggs with
mango chutney and salted cucumber … 84

Pumpkin seeds

Nutty granola with mango compote … 52

Sweet potato hash … 56

R

Rhubarb

Rhubarb crumble waffles … 34

Ribs

Coffee-glazed barbecue short ribs and slaw … 122

Ricotta

Whipped ricotta on sourdough with olive, basil
and sun-dried tomato tapenade … 106

Rocket

Crumpets with slow-cooked portobello mushrooms,
beetroot relish and rocket pesto … 88

S

Sourdough

Creamy mushrooms on toast … 64

Granary sunshine toast … 44

Sacred scrambled tofu … 68

Smoked haddock baked eggs in a
lemon, nutmeg and mustard sauce … 41

Turkish eggs … 48

Whipped ricotta on sourdough with olive, basil
and sun-dried tomato tapenade … 106

White sourdough … 170

Spinach

Sacred scrambled tofu … 68

Smoked haddock baked eggs in a
lemon, nutmeg and mustard sauce … 41

Sweet potato hash … 56

Spring onions

Eggy crumpets with chilli jam and halloumi … 76

Granary sunshine toast … 44

Sweet potato hash … 56

Veggie frittata … 60

Sugar

Anzac biscuits … 134

Blackberry and rose cake … 142

Butternut squash dal with crunchy spiced chickpeas … 118

Coffee-glazed barbecue short ribs and slaw … 122

Cotswold fog … 180

Crumpets with slow-cooked portobello mushrooms,
beetroot relish and rocket pesto … 88

Eggy crumpets with chilli jam and halloumi … 76

Equatorial … 184

Espresso float … 188

Glasrach pizza … 98

Hazelnut caramel slice … 138

Lemon buns … 160

Mile-high lemon meringue pie … 146

Nutty granola with mango compote … 52

Piña colada cake … 130

Rhubarb crumble waffles … 34

Sacred scrambled tofu … 68

Stem ginger cake … 150

Sweet potato hash … 56

Thai yellow eggs with
mango chutney and salted cucumber … 84

The pilot burner … 196

Tiramisu cake … 156

Tiramisu french toast … 72

Sun-dried tomatoes

Glasrach pizza … 98

Whipped ricotta on sourdough with olive, basil
and sun-dried tomato tapenade … 106

Sushi rice

Kimchini … 110

Sweet potatoes

Sweet potato fritters with smashed
avocado, halloumi and poached eggs … 38

Sweet potato hash … 56

T

Tahini

Roasted broccoli with tahini and cranberries … 102

Sweet potato hash … 56

Tofu

Sacred scrambled tofu … 68

Tomatoes

Glasrach pizza … 98

Sacred scrambled tofu … 68

Veggie frittata … 60

W

Walnuts

Courgette and pepper fritters
with beetroot and apple slaw … 94

Y

Yogurt

Nutty granola with mango compote … 52